MW01205249

Spectral Realms

No. 5 ‡ Summer 2016

Edited by S. T. Joshi

The spectral realms that thou canst see
With eyes veil'd from the world and me.

H. P. LOVECRAFT, "To a Dreamer"

SPECTRAL REALMS is published twice a year by Hippocampus Press,
P.O. Box 641, New York, NY 10156 (www.hippocampuspress.com).

Cover art by Harry Clarke for Poe's "The Colloquy of Monos and Una."
Cover design by Barbara Briggs Silbert. Hippocampus Press logo
by Anastasia Damianakos.

ISBN 978-1-61498-181-7   ISSN 2333-4215

Contents

Poems

Borean Soul

Jeff Burnett

Let the vermin scuttle from my path,
Pestiferous and vile, oozing fear,
Or let them stand like men with honest steel—
I'll spike their heads upon a thousand spears.

Let the dragon's lair be my abode,
My flesh baptized in flame and venom-flood;
Let the bones of heroes be my couch;
The dragon be my bride—a bride of blood.

Let the mountains quake with wrath divine
And wingèd things of gibbering maw foretell
A rising cankerworm entitled "God"—
I'll smash him on the frozen lakes of Hell!

Sin Eater

Jennifer Ruth Jackson

Come,
consume the buffet from the body
of the dead.
Delicious finger food nibbled
passes through lips like lies.

Empty
the human table and
absolve the deceased of sin
with every bite—
a baptismal dinner with clergy
absent.

Shove
the soul through heaven's
gates anew, smudging out the hellfire
alighting clothes.

But
make no mistake, no one
covets your seven-course meal.

And
no one will dare touch the tainted food
laid upon you when you are
laid to rest.

The First Haunting

M. F. Webb

We are the infernal, those who fraternize
Unwillingly with shadows, who converse
With wraiths of odd dimensioning, and curse
Our fate. We merely catch each other's eyes,

And nod, and feel no urgency to speak
About the apparitions densely loomed
And clotted in the corners of the rooms
Where we the harried, wraith-beset may meet,

To find some comfort in our comprehension.
The mirrored face, the half-heard dreadful laughter,
The bone-deep sympathy that follows after
Though we may disregard the dead's attention.

We drink to darkness—though that does not serve
To exorcise the hauntings we deserve.

The Second Haunting

M. F. Webb

We know each other at the briefest sight.
The soul-enveloped sickness that enfolds,
Informs each conversation, every glance

Brimmed with remorse, paralysis of chance.
Till lost within the vast familiar night
We relinquish comforts others hold

For half-remembered stories halting told.
Our history is kindred, shared perchance
With eye and breath and shadow, and despite

Desire for warmer friends, simple delight,
We circle still with ghosts, our hands clasped cold
Partners in that wan-complected dance.

The Serpent Borne of Helios

Nathaniel Reed

In the depths of empty space,
Where the cosmic ocean
Laps against the shores of
Nothing, where Life has no
Right to be, where Death is
Not even a word, the Basilisk
Stares out into the void.

A star a billion light-years away
Heaves and cracks, giving way
To darkness, to silence,
To something else:
A hatchling of the abyss
Consumes blackened worlds
Left in blind orbits.

Its nourishment, the heavens,
Gives itself without struggle.
Fangs crack planetary crusts;
Jaws surround Creation itself.
As what is becomes what was,
The Serpent borne of Helios
Coils itself tightly in eternal night.

Coda

Joseph S. Pulver, Sr.

for E. Elias Merhige

Descending. I am one. With no small boat to carry me from this swarm
of flies . . . A prisoner of centuries and sewers . . . .
Rolled in that darkdirt . . . while the worms remembered and sang
the secrets of the labyrinth . . . . every fermentation I cannot
escape . . . .
I remember *The Poet*, the truth of her words.
She sang.
I cried.
I glimpsed. I tasted. I was riddled
The dead came to caution me . . .
She turned away.
Did not laugh,
yet
I could still
taste the damnation
on her tongue.
Left
alone
in that alleyway,
I was
imprisoned,
no vista of Heavenly
to

find stories in.
All
my seas,
ashgrey whores,
a uniform
that
offers Never,
Oblivion—
no heat
no flow
no
pendulum ticket
back to Light,
lost
to the thrust
of a word . . .
Lost.

Lost.

Nothing in this silence unchanging.

Tuesday. Inadequacy.
Then,
challenges
and shifts

bedamned,
the language of the Specter
—*The Poet*,
"Inadequacy."
My
connection with
the rope
is
no longer
confusing

        —*after Ann K. Schwader*

Grin

John J. Mundy

Serpents and Signs
Uncoil in green liquid's fiery hue,
Flecks and streaks of Crimson and Gold
Potent enough to disturb any placid Mask;
Raise now to your lips and drink.
Unique corruption! An anodyne trickle
To Life's Poison! Drink—
The Suns will rise, the black stars shift,
Throats still howl the mad wind.
Now only your mind is stilled fore'er
Behind that idiot's grin.

Graveyards of the Living

G. O. Clark

The dead are visiting
the graveyards of the living,

hospital coma wards
and locked dementia wings;

forgotten alky-alleys
and secret shooting galleries;

front lines of war, and
Humvee caravans out on patrol;

lairs of serial killers
and the homes of murder suicides.

The dead are visiting
the graveyards of the living,

prepared to usher them into
the beyond, when the time is right.

Only in Dreams

Darrell Schweitzer

Only in dreams can I cross that plain
and leave my tracks in trackless dust
of burnt-out suns, and climb those hills
that guard the furthest, deep abyss,
where dead gods and fallen angels lie.

Only in dreams can I slip through time,
into the forbidden yesterday,
converse with crouching demons in
rough-hewn tombs already old
before the Pyramids were young,
and learn such lore that in Atlantis once
a wizard spake to a fear-filled king.

Only in dreams may I trespass
beyond the veil of my own death
and read my words upon a page,
like ancient runes on parchment writ,
and laugh at the mix of terrible truth,
well-stirred with prophecy, nonsense, and dooms.

I know that I must live in dreams,
embrace the madness of the moon,
and in my mind forever shun
the murderous reason of the sun.

The Forest of Horror

Frank Coffman

There is a forest, deep and dread and drear
   In a lost land that few will dare to name,
      A land behind a veil of mystic curse.
The folk who dwell nearby have cause to fear;
   Only the bravest venture in for game
      Just past the wooded edge—for Death . . . or Worse
Awaits any who dare that woodland's heart.
   For something hideous and horrid fey
      Awaits the one who ventures too far in.
The only soul who ever did depart
   From those dire depths . . . he hanged himself that day,
      After a rant on "Evil worse than sin."
Travelers take the long, long way around
   That cursed wood. Some speculate:
      Werewolf? or Wendigo? Demon out of Hell?

This is an expanded "megasonnet" based upon and extruded from the English/Shakespearean pattern. Instead of employing the standard *quatorzain*, it expands the normal quatrains [*abab cdcd efef*] into hexains: [*abcabc defdef ghighi*] and changes the "clincher" couplet [*gg*] into a triplet [*jjj*], resulting in 21 lines.

One of the Old Ones? No trace was ever found
    Of those scant few who dared to test their fate—
        They ne'er returned. They left no tale to tell.

And so, the Haunter of that mystic weald
Remains a fearsome Phantom unrevealed,
A Horror in that Wood's dark depths concealed.

The Egregious Error of Werner Witherbye

John Shirley

He found her as the iris bloomed
and the morning sunlight swelled;
He spotted her as Spring rites loomed
And sighing pines were felled.

She stood upon a hunter's run,
red blooms about her growing;
Her hair gleamed like a dawning sun—
his desire too was glowing.

He doffed his hat, knelt on the sward,
begged the music of her name;
he swore he would draw forth his sword
to protect her from all shame.

Quoth she, "I am called Erizand,
I'm a maid of Sere Legee;
I've seen ought but this forest land—
how I long to know the sea!"

"Maiden, I am Witherbye—
Call me Werner if you please;
I'll escort you low and guard you high
as we journey to the seas."

Her eyes alit, she trusted him,
And they traveled to the west;
they tarried at a lonesome inn:
devils carved upon its crest.

He gave her golden wine to drink
in a goblet he'd prepared;
she felt her heavy head then sink—
his hands upon her hair.

She was no more a maiden
when he'd done his wicked deed;
He was base and he was craven:
when planted he his seed.

But a seed may grow a blossom
or may grow a briar thorn;
and Erizand woke before him,
on that rainy April morn.

Pain and blood awoke him:
and he beheld a demon's claws:
the beast laughing as it choked him,
and gripped him in its paws.

She stroked her scaly demon,
her soft white hands atwitch;
she said, "My foolish young one,
you have soiled a maiden witch.

"To fly far from my family
was e'er my girlish dream;
to flee away from destiny
was my naive scheme.

"Now I know what mortals are,
my fate must be embraced;
but you will scream and you will char,
for all that I'm disgraced."

She instructed her familiar,
an artist at its art;
The cad watched in a mirror
as its blades exposed his heart.

The servants heard the shrieking
and fled into the fields;
the old inn walls were creaking
as if they too would yield.

By parting flesh and cracking bone
was Witherbye revealed;
until his quivering soul alone
was finally unsealed.

Then the demon plucked his soul
like an oyster from a shell;
saw that it was a lump of coal
—to stoke the fires of Hell.

And so ensued the endless doom
for Werner Witherbye;
his suffering woven on the loom
of predatory lies.

Let all men who would deceive
—and think only of their glands—
learn that soon they too will grieve . . .
in the claws of Erizand.

Angry Gods

Mary Krawczak Wilson

When the black holes collide
Their astral sound has gone astray;
I feel reverberations from light-years away
As if I am in Hades and all life has died.

When comets singe the sky
The stars lay flat like crystal stones;
I have seen the celestially strewn bones
Incinerated in the blink of Achilles' eye.

When meteors fall down to earth
Ancient hieroglyphics turn to dust;
I touch the fiery furies from the earth's crust
Only to burn like Icarus and curse my birth.

When the skies darken and fill with ash
The snow is a gritty pipe made of lead;
I taste its metallic cut where I bled
From the sonic bolt that Zeus had crashed.

All Masks Are Mirrors

Ann K. Schwader

All masks are mirrors in the end:
Reflections of some inward scar,
Some pallid truth that we defend.

Beneath black stars, our dreams portend
No future tense. Why seek so far?
All masks are mirrors in the end,

& cracked at that. As cloud-waves blend
Our souls with night, some avatar
Of pallid truth that we defend

Awakes at last. Unmasks. Extends
Its curse to hurl against the stars:
All masks are mirrors. In the end,

Carcosa claims us all, my friend;
Past time for bidding *au revoir*
To pallid truth. That we defend

This specter of our lost lives lends
A certain melancholy—are
All masks but mirrors, in the end?
Some pallid truth that we defend?

The Rime of the Eldritch Mariner

Adam Bolivar

The greatest mercy in the world
    I think is we are blind
To contents that lie tightly furled,
    Asleep within the mind.

Well, it was at a wedding feast
    Where I was next of kin;
A host of fishy relatives
    The church had just gone in,

When did a staring lunatic
    Upon me lay a hand;
His beard grew like a prickly thorn,
    His face in tropics tanned.

It was an Eldritch Mariner,
    Made hoary in short years,
For he had seen with his own eyes
    What lurks in darkest fears.

That is not dead, he raved to me,
    Which can eternal lie.
And æons' strangeness may one day
    Cause even death to die.

It started with a raven that
    Had roosted on the mast.
I tried to disregard its caws,
    Which drove me mad at last.

We sailed in fœtid southern seas,
    In waters thick as ooze,
The constellations alien,
    Our consolation booze.

'Twas on a drunken sleepless night
    That I took up my gun
To shoot the raven through the heart,
    And so the deal was done.

Mayhap it was grim Odin's bird
    That recklessly I'd slain,
And it was then the ocean groaned
    As if it were in pain.

The latitude and longitude
    I'll carry to my tomb,
For it was there a city rose
    Where sleeps our race's doom.

My crewmates' faces turned pale white,
    Just like that maiden Death,
Who kisses you with blood-red lips
    And steals your final breath.

We lit upon the island's shore
    Of slime-slick stones and mud,
And staggered through a ruin that
    Gushed terrors in a flood.

Across the titan masonry
    We crawled like tiny ants;
And what we saw there made us know
    The solace nescience grants.

Vast horrors lay beneath those stones,
    Of that there was no doubt;
Their angles joined impossibly
    To Euclid's theorems flout.

We crossed the courtyard in a daze,
    A monstrous marketplace;
With revelations there we saw
    Our minds could not keep pace.

It was the Portugee who climbed
    That dæmoniac stair
To call us in a hoarsened voice
    With wild dishevelled hair.

A Cyclops' door to hellish depths
    Before us towered high;
To call our actions reasonable
    Would be to tell a lie.

Without result we pushed the door,
    Until the answer dawned:
It hinged on a diagonal—
    And like a maw it yawned.

The aperture was raven-black
    And spewed out horrid things,
Which long had been imprisoned there
    And flew on filmy wings.

The odour was unbearable;
    We heard a slopping sound,
As something lumbered towards the door,
    From far beneath the ground.

Cthulhu now was loose again
    And ravened for delight;
Asleep a vigintillion years,
    Abhorrent was the sight,

For now the stars were right again;
    A mountain stumbled blind—
A sticky star-spawned bat-winged god
    Before us did we find.

And what an age-old cult had failed
    By artiface to do
Accomplished then by accident
    A random foolish crew.

Its flabby claws swept up three men
    Before they even turned;
God rest their souls if there be rest,
    And not from heaven spurned.

We plunged in terror over rocks
    Whose angles most perplexed;
And in the end but two survived
    To witness what came next.

My mate and I fled in the ship
    As fast as she could steam;
The creature cursed us from the shore
    Just like the Polypheme.

The Thing was bold and would not stop;
    It slid into the sea.
The churning claimed my crewmate's mind,
    And soon a corpse was he.

A desperate gamble I took then,
    And so reversed my course
To speed towards the noxious Thing
    And strike with lethal force.

Relentlessly I drove the bow
    Through jelly foul and green,
Which burst and smelt of open graves,
    Abhorrently unclean.

I heard a seething sound astern—
    The sky-spawn recombined;
But our distance widened fast,
    Before I lost my mind.

So now I've told my loathsome tale
    In hopes my soul to shrive;
And yet I fear I shall be cursed
    As long as I'm alive.

Water, water, everywhere,
    Cthulhu dreams below;
R'lyeh wgah'nagl fhtagn:
    This blasphemy I know.

The Weddding-Guest then turned away,
    Made mad from what he'd learned;
And like the Eldritch Mariner
    His soul now heaven spurned.

—From an idea by Robert M. Price

Dark Poet of My Heart

Ashley Dioses

For K. A. O.

With pretty eyes of sapphire I do shine,
Yet there are none that I would have be mine.
They play their tunes with strings inside my heart,
And yet my special love-song makes them part.
With every pull they leave my harp distorted;
When feelings are confessed, theirs are aborted.
Can there be none that would steal me away?
Or do all joy in stealing hearts as play?
Perhaps my heart tires of the songs they pick,
For mine is no mere flame upon a wick.
Perhaps a sound that isn't born of songs—
One filled with words of a good heart that longs.
By quill and parchment I have found the start:
A kindred flame, dark poet of my heart.

Dark House of Hunger

D. L. Myers

The dark window and dark door appear black
Beneath twisted cedars bent like tortured men
That twitch and dance in the growing dusk.
In a pool of lurking shadow, the shack
Squats and waits like a silent toad,
While glints of light shimmer in the liquid jet
Beyond its window panes and broken door.
Upon the sagging porch, piles of bones erode
Into pale grey dust the wind pushes away.
The breeze whispers balefully in the trees,
While the house, crouching like a vulture, groans
And with rabid hunger awaits its prey.

The Ghoul's Dilemma

W. H. Pugmire

I.

O, weary with this world of commonplace,
And stifled by this air of mundane time,
I prick my finger with a pin and trace
Your formula with stain of scarlet slime.
The fragrant stains of crimson slime evoke
A fantasy within the depths of dream
In which I shuffle off this mortal yoke
And enter into nightmare's chilly stream.
Ah, nightmare!—in your graceless revelry
I dance beyond the veil of common things,
I move beyond my mortal brevity,
I fly without the aid of clumsy wings.
Sans wings I spill unto the cosmic pond
And sip the sweet elixir of Beyond.

II.

The dark elixir of this nether-realm
Coils like a cosmic madness out of time.
The maelstroms of my measured language whelm
The chemicals of this daemonic clime.
The Outer Ones that lurk within the dark
Repeat the language of my profane tongue.
Within the blackness I espy a spark
That links me to the spawn of thousand-young.

One thousand young commence to bleat my name
With voices that are laced with mockery.
I know the searing kiss of mortal shame
As once again this husk of normalcy,
This human husk, entraps me in its fit
And I awaken in an earthen pit.

III.
Within this earthen pit I feel my fate
And know what I experienced was dream.
Within this chilly clay I curse and hate
The moonlight that descends as cosmic stream.
I thought I could escape this pit of clay
With language culled from page of antique tome.
I thought I could ascend to dream's array
And so escape embrace of chilly loam.
But no—this hollow pit is my abode,
This yellow bone my dry and drear repast.
My neighbor is the worm, the owl, the toad.
The canine feasters are my ever-caste.
I'll never swim the splendid cosmic flood.
My name is writ eternal in this mud.

The City of Dreadful Life

Richard L. Tierney

In tribute to poet James Thomson (1834–1882)

Dark Bard of Dreadful Night, master of black despair,
Your verses shadow forth the morbid fate
That drives mankind toward that dreaded Gate
Which leads away from pain and woe and care.
Ofttimes we long to pass beyond, yet fear
What might be lurking on the Other Side,
And so in this grim world we yet abide
Beneath its shrouding shadows bleak and drear.

Some curse the God who fashioned this mad City
Of Dreadful Night, while others sense the fate
Of those who know blind Nature's lack of pity.
We yearn to flee this world, yet fear Death's Gate,
And so we grope through gloom and pain and strife
Within this sad, dark City we call Life.

The Resurrection of Death

Gregory MacDonald

A ribcage lay decimated,
wrapped in blood and soil,
half in a broken coffin,
the other encrusted in dirt.
The skeleton's contorted skull
grinned like a fool
as one of its prickly claws
grasped for the sky.
Worms and beetles crawled
over and through its coffin,
as if they were extracting
its bones to build a city,
but as it rose from its black dream,
the creatures fell off alongside the dust.
Next to the coffin was
a crypt candied with frost,
which glittered with the fire of torchlights
guarding both sides of the gateway.
Alit by these torches,
on the top of the tomb's entrance,
were words inscribed in grey stone,
"Do not starve: Subsist on death!"
The spine rolled its head
around and around, like clockwork;
its bone clicked dryly in the process.

It placed on its wan crown
with the use of its frail, pale,
and bony fingers
the necromantic diadem bejeweled
with obsidian stones inside silver locks.
The lich of suicide let out
the shrill shriek of victory
and cackled when the bats observing
from the safety of the crypt rooftop
fled into the haven of night's
protection as the clouds and horizon
closed in with the coming darkling.

The Waves of Fear

Leigh Blackmore

When from the dark there wash the waves of fear
That lave my soul with terrible deep chill,
Forebodings fill me—things that leap and leer.

Throughout this dismal round that forms the year,
The crawling horrors make my soul so ill,
When from the dark there wash the waves of fear.

At midnight leprous, spectral horrors steer
And steal into my home, shudders instill;
Forebodings fill me—things that leap and leer.

My laugh maniacal from there to here
Is heard upon the night-winds near the mill
When from the dark there wash the waves of fear

My mind is cracked, and at itself doth jeer;
It seems a fiendish croucher haunts the sill;
Forebodings fill me—things that leap and leer.

How can I quell disquiet's fraught frontier,
And can I hope to find the strength of will
When from the dark there wash the waves of fear?
Forebodings fill me—things that leap and leer.

Underwater

Ian Futter

Unceasing, unrelenting rain,
pouring down, again, again.
Sploshing, splashing; never stop.
A nation in a water drop.

The timeless tales have all foretold
this Ragnarok; we now behold.
When Thor's great hammer cracks the skies,
in January, to puzzled eyes.

And so begins the onslaught, rank,
where rain drowns rain, from heaven's tank.
And foaming torrent floods the shore
as Aegir rapes the land once more.

While petrol temples brave the cry
from panicked prayers and questions why?
a wave of cars stream from the sea,
but find no ark for you, or me.

Sylvan Blood

Jeff Burnett

I've seen the leper beg on gleaming paves,
Heard the whip-cracks in the hippodrome,
Where nobles, flaunting concubines and slaves,
Flocked to scheme for scepter, crown, and throne:
I'd rather lay my head on mossy stone
And sleep within a tangled wood arcane
Amongst the ebon claws and feral fangs.

I've diced with lowly curs and craven jackals,
Their dainty daggers steeped in viper wine;
I've faced the cut-throats skulking in the shadows
And clove like rotted sticks their brittle spines:
I'd rather war beneath the ancient pines
Against berserker tribes in mountain snow,
Taste the crimson spray of a worthy foe.

I've drunk with bloated kings and pompous priests
Who lounge on velvet, glut from crystal bowls,
Parade in silken plunder from the East,
Whisper treachery in cups of gold:
I'd rather drink hot blood from a dripping skull
And howl to the gods on a mound of conquered dead,
Den with wolves my iron blade has fed.

Myths and Legends

Charles D. O'Connor III

Nobody believes in myths or legends anymore; their beautiful, enchanting melodies have been whisked away like smoke down into somber chasms where broken dreams and bright-eyed dreamers lay scattered amongst ashen streaks of moonlight.

Once these myths and legends ruled our fabled existence with kind, dominant, and upright teachings, aweing our nature with brief glimpses into eternal worlds of wonder and enchantment, chilling our marrow with eldritch beasts and succubi who wait, perched on cobwebbed effigies of gargoyles in darkness, to attack and maim those who wander off into the dens of sin. They've influenced man's belief in himself; and at night, when problems taxed his brain, they fixed his gaze upward, toward oceans of glistening stars, to calm the raging storms.

Now time has passed and cast black shadows of pride over man's eyes. "We know the earth," he bellows. "We know the cosmos. We've studied its stars and learned how it works, how it is born, and when it dies. We create life and we possess the power to end it. We even know what lies beyond its mighty, impenetrable veil. There is no logical or visible evidence to prove myths and legends exist—that's why we refer to them by such names. Man, and only man, exists. We are the highest of all beings—the beginning and the end. Once we die nothing will be important. In fact, everything will follow us."

After finishing his speech, the Scout Master closed the book and looked down at the boys sitting around him, smiling and enjoying the water, flowers, and other gifts that nature was kind enough to bestow upon them.

"What have we learned from this beautiful passage?"

The boys yawned, staring around blankly.

"I don't know," remarked one. "But I do know all legends and myths are false. As the book says, 'that's why we refer to them by such names.'"

The other boys nodded, laughing in agreement.

The Scout Master gritted his teeth. "I'm sorry you boys feel that way and are too blind to see the truth."

Then sweat trickled down his face and purple, pus-filled blisters masked his suddenly ancient features like a rotten mask of death, oozing green, charnel-smelling liquid.

The boys cried, wanting to run, but cold fear paralyzed them.

"Now," he hissed, "I will teach you all about myths and legends."

He tore the book open again with a clawed, wrinkled hand and read passages in a foreign tongue, glancing toward heaven. Every word shot like a cannon from his mouth, cursing and infecting the atmosphere around them—summoning forgotten stories and beings consumed in the whirlpool of time.

The conclusions rippled through the boys' hearts like a frightful memory, but one of them gained enough courage to turn his head and glance up. The beautiful blue atmosphere became darkened, shaping into a titanic tunnel, swirling violently amongst screaming wind, claiming the entire earth as its own like an alpha male.

Slithering sounds soon issued from the opening, and a huge, fetid white worm stuck its slimy head out, observing the world below with red, vengeful eyes. The horrid atrocity growled, revealing sharp, salivating teeth.

Before the boys could react, the white worm pounced down upon the earth for a brief second, engulfing them all; their screams muffled by the sounds of crunching bones and spurting blood, which stained the grass like red paint on canvas.

And with that the Scout Master read passages in another tongue, the worm returned to its home, the wind calmed, and the sky resumed its brilliant blue hue. All was peaceful once again.

Meanwhile, across the water, propped against a willow, was an artist named Dr. Robert Thornton. He finished adding color to the worm, the boys, and the flowers. Then he examined the flowers he'd finished, admiring their beauty and meditating on olden songs, and returned to the city with dreams of becoming a botanist.

Beyond the Stones

Liam Garriock

My Love, dost thou not remember
    The golden glade when we held hands
    And danced to the tune of fey bands
One shining day in September?

We wedded in the stone circle
    That our ancestors erected,
    Where life has aye been protected;
Thy fair head was crowned in myrtle.

The fauns and the gods were our guests,
    Our priest the priest of sleeping Pan,
    And I—I was the dreaming man
Whose sanctuary was thy breasts.

And now thou art forever gone.
    The Druids and the gods long dead,
    The magic of the stones hath bled
Dry, and with them I stand alone.

Perchance ere the end of all things,
    The ghosts of old gods and faeries
    Dance in the fading summer breeze,
And in the heart the Goddess sings.

Cast Away

Oliver Smith

A hundred gray-green seas washed me here
Where the pelican floated a shadow on the sky.
I sat lonely and broken beside the bay.
He waited wise and silent in his gray robe,
The witness to my exile on these yellow sands.

I was caught among driftwood, nails, weed,
Bright pebbles bladder-wrack, sea lettuce,
Cockle shells, coral, fish bones, and sorcery;
Gulls, fireflies, green lizards, disembodied spirits,
Oak, cypress, cedar, and turpentine trees.

On the jagged island birds' eggs abounded:
I gorged for a week on the raw yellow feast,
As the pelican scooped silver fish from a pool
And a stranger watched from a broken pine.
She was a fine skull hung in the branches.

Signs carved in the wood declared her witch
And beyond ivy grew over the unmortared blocks
Of an enchanted palace. Deep in indigo shadows
I found her star-fused portrait from a time
Before she grew to nought but bones.

She was silk robed, embroidered, and dressed
Gleaming metal and frosted jewels: a living machine.

She seemed built of fragments, flux, lost scraps
Pearls, diamonds, gold, pine, moss.
The name, Miranda, was engraved on her ivory case.

I found only the thinnest barrier of years separated us.
A little time on the ocean, a little time among the stars,
A little time rotting in the sun's heat and hurricanes blast.
In cool shaded rooms I heard the tread
Of a pretty silken boot.

There was the swish of her farthingale in the grass
And sweet laughter among the turpentine trees.
Enchanted by her shadow she told me of means
To enflesh her bones. So I brought before her
Fish, lizards, rats fled from a certain shipwreck

Sailors released from abyssal storage, babes in arms,
Kings, bishops, toilers in the dirt, tavern keepers,
Angels, murderers, saints, second-hand booksellers,
And as many typesetters as I could muster.
With each offering a little more meat returned

To her bones: another bloodstain on her fingers,
A scrap of fair or freckled skin, a lock of reddest hair
Until at last she stood a queen reborn.

The pelican floated frozen in a motionless arc:
A ghost of old Prospero caught in the wind.

Miranda sat sucking lighting from the storm
Bound me in chains forged from her iron
Heart in the heat of the fire in her blood.
She who consumed the flesh
Of men then named me her cannibal.

A thousand fates bore me to this island
Where the pelican rules as a guiding star
And the witch Miranda leads me on a chain.
This monster in her robe of sea-green silk,
Made me her slave on these yellow sands.

Me

Ross Balcom

by a process
dim

I found
myself

in a manse
remote and lost

I walked
the halls

doors dissolved
at my touch

I saw my face
in a window

a demon
with a fool's grin

I ran
from the place

but there was no escape
from me

I was flashing
everywhere

like lightning

Dies Irae

Carole Abourjeili

The day of wrath I you bestow
The hour *Israafyil* shall blow
The deafening trumpet he proclaims
The dooming stars sentenced to flames
Holy Myriam shall then kneel
Her earnest heart my soul shall heal
Her moaning soul
The sinful Dame
'Quench your soul with all my shame'
The heavenly kingdom shall descend
My fearing eyes
My healings end
My tainted sins I shall admit
My drunken soul I then submit
Quench my spirit amid your light
Absolve my sins with all your Might
Summon my soul to your right.
Your Holiness, thus earth did make
Thus all your creatures shall awake
The Star of David shall once bend
To form a cross then, a crescent
The trumpet blown a second spell
Ashes and Demons thus befell
The tearing blood the earth possessed
The ending time has been confessed.

The Alchemist's Disease

Nathaniel Reed

Age has crept upon me while I have answered others' questions though my own remain: Charon's obol may be paid through tricks, yet my desire flames to escape doom on this mortal plane. The iron veins of the earth run with amber blood, but the flesh pulses crimson with something much beyond; for the secrets of stones and metals from the womb below mean nothing when the Material of Life is a secret still entombed!

Or so I said as I set about the search for what cannot be found in shafts that spider through the earth. . . .

Rituals and conjurations written in blackened grimoires for which I sent led me no closer though they hinted at such as I should come to find. Cowardly priests told me to repent. Libraries across this dread-filled world locked their doors to me. By even the most Stygian of scholars I found myself maligned. Those I once called truest friends turned their backs until at last I saw and heard no more from those death-bound kind.

And so I searched miserably alone: to give oneself to forbidden study is to stalk madness where it hides, though it was in the cacophony of the void where the answer lie. . . .

Even now I hear the never-fading sounds of the endless corridors which circle and surround! From those hell-bred tunnels, some nameless thing gave to me what I called eternal blessing yet now I call disease. For destitute of the Life I held deep within my sacred flesh, forever do I haunt this sphere of saving Death! I beg of whoever hears my pleas, wish not for more than that Seeming Curse of Mortality!

So say I, the dust of a world which forever orbits on, as nothing can release me as the endless cycles come. . . .

Transylvanian Darkness

K. A. Opperman

The wolves howl out in primeval hunger,
The wind blows coldly, caressing
The red gown of a bride who for beauty had died
In the black, Transylvanian darkness.

By woodlands old when Time was much younger
I pace, forever obsessing
Over lost Nevermore, in this graveyard of yore
In the black, Transylvanian darkness.

The vampire plagues this province, forsaken
Of God, and shunned by the village—
But my blood has grown chill, and my heart all but still,
In the black, Transylvanian darkness.

Blue flames on cursed Walpurgis awaken
Where lies old Dacian pillage,
But my treasure long lost fills a grave over-mossed
In the black, Transylvanian darkness.

A castle stands whose ruins will never
Forget a romance medieval . . .
Where the wild rose entwines under Luna's white tines
In the black, Transylvanian darkness.

The Land Beyond the Forest forever
Enslaves my soul to its evil
'Neath Carpathian spells in this hell of all hells,
In the black, Transylvanian darkness.

Temple of the Flame

David Barker

Numbed and saddened by the savage brutality of this Earth's ruling cultures, I long for the lush jungle lands of a distant world where the ancient smoldering fires of an eldritch sun spawn fantastic, unheard-of life forms: fauna and flora of every imaginable hue and configuration, strange hybrids unique to a mad, spinning, insular galaxy. I know with inexplicable certainty that there I would find the vaulted granite temple wherein legions of blind and smiling stone effigies squat hideously before the eon-spanning flames of immemorially burning altars—mute and smug, their primal, archetypal secrets safe behind the impenetrable veil of a thousand centuries of accumulated stellar dust and the crumbling oblivion of an empire of pillaged planets. Wandering through the vast silent halls for hours, my footprints disturbing the virginal corridors and tableau'd passageways, my astonished fingers tracing the graven scenes of former grandeur that hint of scientific wonders and aesthetic accomplishments far beyond the ken of mankind, I know I would rediscover the sense of cosmic wholeness I have long since lost on this pathetic globe. Someday, when the key has been revealed that will unlock the gateway, I will make this voyage, and after I have conferred with those icons in the Temple of the Flame, I will journey out upon the broad, time-worn migratory route past the realms of the setting sun, to dwell forever in the legendary kingdom of the Elder Gods.

The Sayings of the Seers

Wade German

They came to share what others could not see,
To spread the sayings of their analects—
The eyeless visitors from off-world sects
Who sensed with witch-sight things that should not be;
Who spoke of beings that had always been
Outside dimensions limiting our own;
Of truth and wonders hitherto unknown
That through their sayings all could now be seen.

And men were eager for a higher world.
Those ancient warlocks met with human scribes
To gift their gospels to the chosen tribes—
Then hatred flourished, genocides unfurled
As verse and chapter spoken to enslave
The souls which haunt this world become a grave.

Antagonist

F. J. Bergmann

After Kelli Hoppmann's Adversaries III, *oil on panel, 2013*

Dawn's eye opens a silent pulse of scarlet.
Your skull swivels to stare backward
into unrelieved morning, the carnal past.
A clatter of black wings. You inhale decay,

aromatic vapor rising from rotting carrion
like a mordant into the red-dyed sky,
and store it for later use. You can fly in light
or shadow, become your own dark army.

Noon sunbright on snow: a windform spins,
its whirl of glitter masking your bootprints.
The black dog always bounding at your side.
leaves no tracks. You will walk him again

at midnight, when your nightshine feathers
quiver to moonbeat and harbor the negative
of radiance. You savor that, also, and inflate
a repugnatorial organ with a rush of blood.

The fear you instill is a road, not a destination.
Where will you go after the long, long war?

Heaven in Your Arms

Jennifer Ruth Jackson

We move together, you and I,
in this dance we have no name for,
with no melody to underscore our
punctuating footfalls.

You place your arms around my neck
and I wear you like jewelry.
Your brazen move shall
leave its mark upon me.

I can no longer catch my air.
My eyes close when you stop and
hold me tight as if you loved me still,
and were not choking me to death.

Season Spirits

Juan J. Gutiérrez

I. Lantern

O foolish fire, encased in lantern skin,
Bleed out this night and light my way
With elemental grin.
Reveal the Horns of Deviltry,
Show me the Mask of Death;
I'll gaze beyond the dead-grin glow,
Beyond the dead-leaf flesh.

Darkling, by autumn-magic gloom,
The dead arise and glow again
By ghostly lantern's bloom.
Enmasked by blackened goblin cheer,
Revealed to those who know,
The secret of All-Hallow's shine
In arcane songs of crow.

O foolish fire, cast thy golden decay;
Each step I take, in darkened paths,
Unveils a guised ballet.
Hordes of laughing demons, running,
Burning autumn leaves,
Cackle, scream, and shout their tricks,
While mourners bow to grieve!

II. The Demon of Golden Decay

There is a dark and golden fiend
In October, only dreamed;
It spreads convivial wonder and fear,
With a grin but once a year.

Lo! the demon of golden decay,
Creeping by lantern display,
Following the masked, laughing child,
Enthralled by the season, beguiled,

When the pumpkin light screams,
It retreats to your dreams,
Waiting for your wistful, autumn call,
When the gold leaves shall fall . . .

Fallow Fields

Mary Krawczak Wilson

For years now it all lies flat,
Amber-hued and yellowed with age;
Ophidians languish in the scrub and the sage;
No sign of a mouse nor a shrew—not even a rat.

Once it was lush, radiant and gold,
Moist and mossy, verdant and green;
Far from the deciduous trees yet seldom even seen
Except by the visionaries—both wizened and old.

The fields were full of jasmine, lilac, and heliotrope,
And the air danced and dazzled in the light;
Heady flowers perfumed the world at night;
It was an idyllic land of beauty, eternity and hope.

Now it is all no more—it is decimated;
Nothing but an empty chasm reeking of death.
Even the insects have taken their last breath,
For long ago the mortal gods conceived their fate.

Redux

John J. Mundy

I am the mask behind the flesh;
The hungry flesh behind the mask.
I am a universe of ill will
In a black medical bag.
I am the crawling shame of Heaven,
God's most grievous, secret Sin.
I am the fog-born shriek,
Gnashing and ripping shark's teeth—
I am a night ocean of blood.
I am your crimson nightmare,
Your black bloated leech.
I am the dream you fear
(The one that will never leave at dawn).
I am the shadow of your dread—
The outsider inside you bred;
I am the living—
Are you now the dead?
That scalpel in our hand—
Is it yours, my Jack? Or mine?

Death and a Locket

Jonathan Thomas

Death came for me on a wet April night,
Charcoal suit, yellow teeth, yellow tie.
He smelled of cologne over mildew and dust,
And asked was I ready to die?

Of course I said no, and he offered a deal,
With his skeletal smile cold and sly:
I could name him a loved one to go in my place,
And the thought of you then made me cry.

He lit a cigar, said he'd sweeten the deal,
That I needn't come out and decide,
That if I permitted he'd guess my decision,
And with silence was how I'd comply.

He gave me some seconds that did me no good;
I could not bring myself to reply,
And he took that for answer as I feared he would
And I trembled at thinking you'd die.

He snuffed the cigar and suggested your name
And asked me if you'd qualify,
But I told him no, that I didn't love you,
While I tried looking him in the eye.

He didn't dispute me, just smiled hungrily,
And told me to let my tears dry.
What I'd asked for was done, and he took out a locket
And commanded me to look inside.

I expected your picture, I was full of self-hate,
But it seemed I had done well to lie,
For the face of a stranger was opened to me,
And your life I'd been able to buy.

But death sat too calmly, asked was I surprised,
Did I wonder whom I'd caused to die?
When I called him a stranger I'd seen once or twice,
His laugh made my throat turn bone-dry.

"In all the wide world, this one loved you the best,
Though now you will never know why,
And his life he gave freely, which is something that you
Or your love seem ill-suited to try."

Death left me then, but he's never seemed far,
And at what seemed deep feelings I sigh,
And now I don't know what to do about us,
Or the love whose truth death has defied.

The Endless Night

Christina Sng

The night grew deep into our eyes,
Gum thick with weariness.
We lay like little children,
Looking out at eternity

Through four-inch-thick glass,
Wrapped up in our blankets
For a camp out under the stars.
A final night out.

Our mothership was
Dead in the vacuum.
We had failed. Humanity
Would soon be extinct.

My eyelids fluttered open
One last time, one instant.
A sliver of light.
No, just imagination.

Then the gentle free fall.
Almost forever. Reminding me
Of lights glinting off
The crystalline water,

As we leapt into the waterfall
Laughing, screaming, and
We soared, high on Papa's shoulders
At the rainbow-coloured carnival,

Two peas in a pod,
Ecstatic with delight,
Clambering onto the platform
Where we rode those brightly

Painted wooden horses
Prancing placidly around,
Going nowhere. And everywhere.
The mirrors blurred us all.

Night caught us again,
Placed us gently into
Our Mama's safe warm arms,
Rocking us to sleep,

Then stopping suddenly
Almost forever
Before we soared again
With a gentle grace.

I had to know.
The sensors picked it up. Visual.
We were on an enormous wing,
Several miles long, on glide.

I turned the camera to the body:
It was a grey streamlined form
With four enormous wings
Propelling it through space,

Guided by thousands
Of bright silver eyes,
Each the size of a small moon,
Encasing the front of its head.

I crawled to her side,
Held her cold hands,
Pressing them to my lips.
Her eyes were silver, frozen.

"Mama, you were right!"
I whispered in her ear.
"The Leviathans are real!
We are riding on its wing."

She did not have to say anything;
The stars in her eyes said it all.
I lay in my mother's arms, letting
Happy memories of the carnival

Flood my head, flashing
Psychedelic colors,
The brightest I'd ever seen.
They washed away the darkness,

Filled my eyes
With pure incandescent light.
I opened them forever
And smiled farewell to the night.

An Existence

Ian Futter

What might this have been
in another life?
This chaos of cells,
this blood sack of strife?

When might this spirit
have leapt over worlds,
catching calm, cooling stars
like a cluster of pearls?

When might these bones
have been braces, afire,
blazing out from the dark
of eternity's spire?

What might these ears
have heard in the hush,
when a trillion mouths moved
and were soundlessly crushed?

What might these fingers
have touched through the years,
from the searing first sun
to the grave's growling gears?

Oh, what wonders these eyes
might have finally seen
had they not been clamped tight
to this counting machine.

The Cold Fog of Regret

John Shirley

It's that time in December
when one tries not to remember
all the dismal chambers of the mind.
And one strolls past twisted oaks
to pause where blackened marble's choked
with greedily relentless scarlet vines.
In the grip of thickening mist,
we try to grasp what went amiss;
we search for something finer there to find.

But mist here never dissipates,
nor softens to a warmer state
(nor does it form meteorologically).
The soul that drifts here enervates,
taking on the chilling local traits
(some claim it's trapped astrologically).

For this fog is made of memories,
of depleted spirit energies:
in essence, it distills regret.
So though you're seeking here to hide,
it takes you only back inside—
where early errors are persisting yet.

Postcard from the Night Desert

G. O. Clark

Late at night, the bats
suck nectar from the saguaro cactuses,
like vampires from the necks
of prickly old maids.

Some fallen saguaros,
ribs highlighted by the full moon's glow,
litter the ground like dead vaqueros
after a barroom brawl.

Darkness, death, and
things that slither dot the parched desert
landscape, along with tiny lizards dreaming
their velociraptor dreams.

Ancient eyes follow the
midnight tourist, tooth and claw eager
to tear into tender flesh; discarded skeleton
left to bleach in the sun.

Other Humans

Gregory MacDonald

Creeping mist crawled
over the graveyard.
A woman dressed in black cried,
"Life is too hard.
I would that I were dead!"
In the dark trees observed
lycans licking their lips,
relishing the mortal pain,
which they have
never sincerely felt,
as they relish
their bloodthirsty fame.
The moon quaked
and a deluge of light
ousted all the hidden creatures;
they self-consciously scuffled
into the last vestiges of night while
the woman wept crystals onto
the gravestone of her beloved.
The mist crept a little closer,
as did the shuffling shadows
feeding on her sorrow.

The Festival

Chad Hensley

I pursued cowled and cloaked silent figures;
A frosted forest led to hoary church.
The ancient place was filled with weird whispers;
Peculiar shapes peered from ceiling's high perch.

Somewhere inside, a chiseled staircase led
Spiraling down in damp, stinking darkness
To sunless beach that filled me with great dread
For lurid, queer lights moved in the farness—

Sickly, green fire hiccupped nasty, thick smoke.
The faceless throng clasped hands around the flames.
From foul waters, flopping, winged things did croak
With human mouths, they shouted godless names.

Then the encircled crowd pulled down their cowls.
I ran with fear, chased by inhuman howls.

The Summons

D. L. Myers

There is a grim, fog-shrouded forest
Beyond the confines of my room,
That whispers of its grottos
And hisses of its dooms.
It calls me with a purpose
That is masked and so obscure—
My mind's aswirl with wonder
At the dark and sweet allure
Of this place of wicked beauty
That seeks some unknown boon
From my mind and trembling body
Beneath the misty winter moon.
And deep within its vastness
I will find a sacred space
Where my wonder will be answered
And my fate I shall embrace.

A Traveler to the City

Frank Coffman

Of late, I see that city in my dreams—
    Or rather Night Terrors—for there is no peace!
        It rises from my sleep's abyss: a Horror!
        But I have seen that dreadful place before—
    Long years ago—and I had sought release!
But rosaries, confessions full, it seems
A lasting succor failed! That city gleams
    Under strange moons; the twin suns cease
        Their rounds; the cloud waves break along the shore.
        It looms, with broken spires and streets of gore,
    With winged things flying, as the winds increase.
And from the city's depths a strange light beams!

Oh there! The king who wears the yellow tatters
    Sits throned, and, round about him, howling, lies
        A throng of awful minions, nine times nine.
And through those eldritch paths, the pads and patters
    Of cosmic creatures sound; and hideous loud sighs
        Of those, though long dead, do not yet resign
Themselves. Alas! I've read the tome that matters!
    And anyone who reads that cursed play dies!
        This jewel—my gold-etched onyx—the Yellow Sign!

This is a Petrarchan/Italian "Megasonnet" (the traditional form expanded from 14 to 21 lines rhyming: abccbaabccba / defdefdef).

Fallen Atlantis

Ashley Dioses

For D. S. F.

It must have been a wonder to behold
The fallen city of Atlantis old.
Huge abalones gleamed in sapphire waves,
With opal glints reflecting off their cold
And glossy surfaces from shallow caves.

The pillars were of pearl, the cracked old floors
Contained red streams of coral; in the doors,
The orichalch, a pallid flame-gold hue,
Bedazzled the aquatic rooms through pores
And fissures in the palace painted blue.

It was now home to hoards of Merish folks,
The selkies and the kelpies, and their croaks
And squabbles over broken homes and food.
The languid sirens teased the men as strokes
From nacre combs groomed tresses gold-imbued.

Mari Lwyd

Liam Garriock

Down among the villages I go,
To the doors of the folk, singing
Our sacred songs, my bells ringing
As I dance and sway to and fro.

My friends they sing with valour, pride
In our native land, without fear
As we walk into the New Year
And stand loyally by my side.

Cold is the night, but warm my friends,
For they stand by me, undaunted
By the darkness and its haunted
Hills where dwell the small folk and fiends.

Life and Death, and birth and rebirth,
There is no gate between the two;
All are cyclical, of the new
Seasons that dawn upon the earth.

Down among the villages I go,
To the doors of the folk, singing
Out sacred songs, my bells ringing
As I dance and sway ere the snow.

In Nether Pits

David Barker

A thousand steps
beneath the loam,
in nether pits
the ghouls call home,
I spied a face
I thought I knew,
a long dead friend
all gone to grue.

Thus startled in
his native clime,
he fast withdrew
to shade and slime,
but not before
I thought I saw
a severed limb
grasped in his paw.

I thought to draw
him from the gloom
into the light
of that deep room
where hoary crypts
are stacked three deep
and subterranean
rivulets seep.

He would not quit
his hiding place,
would not reveal
his decayed face,
shrank from the torch's
lurid glow,
abhorred the truth
the light would show.

Memories fond of
days long past
compelled I save
this sad outcast,
or if he prove
beyond salvation,
dispatch him to
overdue damnation.

But as I crept
to where he lingered,
from all around my
coat was fingered,
then clutched, then ripped
by digits rotten—
a dozen hands
tore at the cotton.

Then I fast fled
that sunken room,
raced up the steps
and quit the tomb.
The ghoulish horde
were at my heels,
their arms reached out
like writhing eels.

Yesterdawn

Jeff Burnett

Caryatids cast down the cumbering heft
Of centuries; a pulverizing pall
Cloaks the broken eidola strewn and sprawled
Repulsively voluptuous in death.

Noctis nymphs of callipygian frame
Bear the seal of mordant lichens black;
Priapic demigods demoniac
Of votive gold and silver fall defamed

On shattered flags usurped by swaying grass.
Metallic torsos shed aeruginous limbs,
Senesce to mottled wreckage fungi-dim,
Heaped like monstrous insects wrought of brass.

Faceless figures merge with hoary soil:
Probing roots with porphyry idols wed,
Languid vines molest the precious dead
Of fabled epochs; deathly silence coils

About the fallen Satyr and the Faun—
Their orgies (frozen in the marble frieze)
Flake away as autumn-scattered leaves,
Marmorean tetter filming Yesterdawn.

Dancer

Christina Sng

Dancer twirls
Like a runaway top
Spinning through space
Into the void beyond.

She's learnt to halt
Her breathing till she
Reaches her next stop,
Where she consumes everything.

We've found galaxies
She's passed through,
Energy signatures ebbing
Like fading songs.

In her millions of cycles
As a Star Chaser
And a Bounty Hunter,
Bella has never encountered

A black hole that can
Control its own power.
Most simply devour all matter
Caught past their event horizons.

But Dancer is no ordinary black hole.
She is sentient and in complete control.
It will take all of Bella's wits
And cunning to capture her.

There are rumours that Dancer
Is the only known roaming gateway
To other worlds, a priceless power
On the intergalactic black market.

Bella discovers this is true
When she is whisked into
An alternate universe where
She is just an ordinary girl.

In that timeline, Bella
Watches her doppelgänger live
A very different life from hers
While she hunts Dancer in spurts,

Distracted by the potential
This other Bella girl demonstrates:
Growing up in a family, pets,
Work, marriage, children, death.

And when Bella finally
Has Dancer in her grasp,
She does not say farewell
To her other self,

Born in a different universe
To a different mother,
Living a very different
Existence from hers.

A simpler one. The joy etched
On her visage as she feels
The presence of something
Familiar yet untouchable.

A peace Bella has never felt before.
But now she will think of it no more,
Focusing instead on the capture at hand.
Through the wormhole she traverses,

Piercing antimatter hooks into
Dancer's side as she emerges
In her own universe,
Energy signature confirmed.

Dancer is dragged by hooks into
A prison specially made for black holes,
Sealed forever in the Singularity Jar,
And handed over to the Elders.

It is another successful mission
For Bella, but the memory
Of her other self
Will haunt her forever.

Alive

Joseph S. Pulver, Sr.

ALIVE
with storms
my wings in Tomorrow
the chains of mundane clay-appetites no longer
                    lapping at my heels.
Starry within
—beneath The Mask—
awakened
risking everything
I, a house taken over,
danced
unashamed
invited to patterns of Undoing.

Origins

Nathaniel Reed

Hidden in marshes near the wild
Shores of barren and windswept dunes
Above a dying world, I came to know
Of nameless things bound to another
Earth before, where primordial oceans
And glacial monoliths once shaped
And scarred the distant past long
Since drowned in lost, forgotten depths.

As the sky turned gray, the sound of
Gusts joined in chorus with the waves,
And I walked upon a swale ringed by
Lichen-eaten sentinels whose surfaces
Seemed to melt and flow in hideous patterns.
Compelled by silent voices in my mind,
I stalked to the center of the pit
Marked by a single standing stone.

Moving as the others though
With wholly different shape,
Like a phantasm sculpted by the
Winds and rains of endless age,
I reached an arm to feel its face,
Seeing in its lines cursed words
Gone unspoken since
The dust of creation settled into Life.

The stench of eons of decay took hold;
Turning back my gaze, I stumbled
And collapsed into the putrid mud.
Scar-red rays filtered through the clouds;
Transformed, the world took on hues
No human eye should ever see.
The rain began to fall, an acrid torrent
Steaming as it struck the earth.

But the horrid storm was nothing
Compared to the things that reached up
From below, their pale bodies convulsing,
Featureless faces and limbless shapes,
Nightmarish shades of living things,
That, in some grotesque revelry,
Danced as the reeking ichor poured
Around their awful, grotesque forms.

The things converged together,
Rising up from the earth in sacrilege
To the heavens lost beyond.
Their shifting outline coalesced
Against the alien horizon as I stared
For eternal, anguished moments until
Madness took me as its own, for the
Shape was the same as that strangest stone.

Flowing as they had before,
Those living glyphs spoke to me
In silent voices that echoed
Through my broken mind,
Reeling back I cried and prayed
"Death strike me here, where I lie!"
For what I saw crawl from those lines
Were shapes much too like our humankind!

Atu II: The High Priestess

Leigh Blackmore

O maiden high, the goddess Silver Star!
Pan's bride, the Mother of the world you are!
Eternal virgin, blessings unto you,
The Veil through which effulgent Light shows through.
That luminous Veil, that brilliant dazzling ray
Is there to guide us on our journeying way.
Most pure exalted Lady, Angel-bright
Administer all beings with Sound and Sight.

Isis you are, with child clasped to your breast;
And Artemis you are, her huntress bow at rest.
Formless effulgence—crystals, pods, and seeds,
All nascent life—enchanted now proceeds.

O Gimel-Camel path, grant us your Kiss—
Under the Lunar Goddess all is Bliss!

Visitor

Fred Phillips

When darkness over Bekra drew its veil
Some movement was discerned that had not been
By any living being ever seen,
Or rendered in some long-forgotten tale.
A shape, manlike, a shadow slowly slid
Darker than the living night could hold,
A presence that would terrify the bold
To wreak whate'er a higher Power bid.
To market in its ancient timeless square
Once Ra again revealed his shining face,
'Twas not what had once been a crowded place,
But of man's presence curiously bare,
And Bekra to which once was commerce led
Is no more than a city of the dead.

The Fetch

John J. Mundy

It lay cramped between a graveyard's borders
And the burned-out shell of a deconsecrated church;
The rotting roof sagged perilously,
The windows blear or broken,
The lawn overgrown, weeds waist-high.
No one had lived there for years . . .

One gray twilight, passing, I spied a man
Pacing the warped, weathered porch boards.
His eyes were terrible, his face frightful,
His visage corroded by the black acids of time
And a smoldering demonic hate.
Suddenly, his pale figure halted; he turned
To appraise me—such a look of gloating malice!
He seemed Insubstantial, a mere ghostly trace—
How I wish he hadn't worn my face!

R'lyeh

F. J. Bergmann

Dreaming, an ancient entity twitches in its sleep,
Sleeps deep beneath the veils of age and dust.
Dust falls in silence in the Eldest House.
Housed in stone like a brain within a skull,
Skulking in the passages of thought,
Thoughtless, near-insensate—yet it lives,
Lives upon lives in universe after universe,
Versed in rituals transcending space and time.
Time for the conjunction of the darker stars,
Stars come right at last for Cthulhu, dreaming.

Whisper

Oliver Smith

He waits whisper-thin in the gateway
Where two moons fall forever tracing
Spirals in the shrunken sky; they hurtle
Over blasted deserts and bloody sands
Mined deep by splintered wings
Shed in the flight of a midnight star.

Temple-columns stand half-buried
On the rim of a retreated sea
Worn to stubs by a billion years
In the roar of storms and cry of wind
That long ago faded: a murmur
In the waning air.

A forgotten rumour rises on lips
Of dead clay and memory. Broken ghosts
Of the first creation stretch hungry
Tongues from shadowy burrows:
Haunters who forgot the haunted
Rotted to nothing in the ground.

In younger incarnations
Their race declared how fertile,
How fruitful, how rich this Earth
Where towers resonated in bright
Counterpoint to the melody
Of rivers, seas, and shoreline.

His words are dry and worn as history
Hidden in the drifts of rusted sand.
Lost in the land of stone and iron
Where the young worlds lush green song
Has worn to tuneless sepia, leaving
Only dust and bone.

Beauty's Veil

Gregory MacDonald

The maenad hovered silhouette at a stormy sky's zenith;
her whole form was as if disharmonic music
had formed a body for a brief moment:

beauty is not a beauty at all, the blood makeup failed
to cover skinless patches under her sewn scarred nipples;
her iridescent eyes betrayed blindness to evolving spirit;

tamed and chained wild hounds panted at her voluptuous thighs;
serpents seethed as her hair and the air around her rippled
like atmospheric events tempestuous and destructive—

nature's aesthetics which paralyze our zeal for life.
I must revere her conquering of things temporal with haste—
for there is an ominous shape behind her. Beauty is not veiled;

she is the veil hiding the darker doom deeper
in despair, fears dormant and unconscious.
Don't avert your gaze, don't be too curious,

settle for beauty and her forms, for what's behind is more than death,
more than annihilation, but blank, oh terrifying blank, hollowness
    unfurled,
like a nightmarish cloud hovering over the imagination.
The nothingness behind her is an ancient archon draining all life as a tax.

Ever Fair

Ashley Dioses

Your hair of onyx, ever fair,
Has gained the scent of sweetest pear.
Your skin of pallid roses slips
To ghoulish green and ice blue hips.
Your lips of softest petals kiss
My lips no more, no more, yet hiss
In whispers like the wind when I
Submerge your body in the lye.

Agents of Dread

David Barker

I have heard the ghost children
laughing down through night's depths,
long after midnight sighs,
when a mournful wind
carries their feral scent to me,
and in terror I have shuttered my windows
and marked the door posts and lintels
with ruddy sigils to bar their entrance,
and yet still they arrive, two
emaciated young girls with stringy hair
and pale, ashen skin,
garbed in decayed raiments,
begging admittance with
fey voices and dead obsidian eyes,
appealing to my sympathetic instincts,
singing "Oh sir, we hunger
and it is time to feed!" and
"Let us in, sir! We are cold and
your chamber exudes warmth!" But
I do not give in to this demonic pair;
I remain vigilant, for
I have viewed the ghastly remains
of kindhearted innocents

who made the fatal error
of unbolting their doors and
letting in fiends who would
feast on bodies and souls
in the guise of benign children
with ebony eyes and
razor-sharp teeth.

Classic Reprints

The Song of the Sea

Edgar Saltus

O what are you trying to tell me,
    Great Elemental of blue?
I hear your insistent voice calling
    In tones but known to the few.
Are you sighing for lost Atlantis
    And mysteries of the deep,—
Or like an enveloping mother
    Are you singing me to sleep?

Are you singing of far, fair islands
    Of azure, coral and light,
Where the palm trees droop to your kisses
    In a land of warm delight?
Will you bear me on sun-tipped billows
    To isles of enchantment, where
The glory of God is bursting forth
    In brilliance everywhere?

Will you clasp and bathe and enfold me
    Down in your passionless deep,
Where the long lithe arms of the Undines
    Will gather me in to sleep?

Will you wash and cleanse me and purge me
    From the memory of pain—
And then roll me up on the seashore
    To begin my life again?

[Taken from Saltus's *Poppies and Mandragora* (New York: Harold Vinal, 1926). Text provided by Henry J. Vester.]

Voodoo

Annice Calland

Ho, the pan-pipes call to Bassin Bleu
To dance the dance of the great voodoo;
The big drums boom, the conch shells blare,
The signal fires flame and flare;
Oh-o-ay-o-eyah, the strange songs sound
While the dancers gather at the singsing ground.
The tympani louder and louder boom,
Echoing far their song of doom;
Oh-o-ay-o-eyah, the wild songs seem
The echo of the conchs' scream.
Ho, the pan-pipes call to Bassin Bleu
To dance the dance of the great voodoo!

And ever the great drum beat, and beat,
And ever the woman sang.

The voodoo priest came looming near,
A piece of shell in each black ear;
On his wizard's skull aigrets and plumes,
(Ever the great drum beating, booms),
About his neck as black as jet
White bone and shell and metal met;
About his legs it clinked and wound
Like a slithering serpent there unbound.
Painted and decked the witch-priest stood

Among his people in the singsing wood.
The full moon flooded the place with light
Yellow, misty, strangely bright.
A low chant rose from the singsing ground,
And in and out and through they wound;
They took their places, legs spread wide,
They stood like statues side by side.

And ever the great drum beat, and beat,
And ever the woman sang.

Voices and instruments sudden ceased,
Only the voice of the drum increased;
Stirred by the booming the big drum made,
To its savage rhythm the voodooists swayed.
The witch doctors formed a circle about
The voodoo priest who in and out
Whirled like a dervish in the wheel
Of the lecheurs swirling toe and heel.
Again the chant, now soft and low
In regular tempo clear and slow;
The voodoo priest still whirling led
To the slower rhythm, whirling sped
Swifter and swifter as the rhythm grew fast
His violence grew until at last

Contorted, twisted, a half crazed thing
He squatted, spent with his spell-making.

And ever the great drum beat, and beat,
And ever the woman sang.

All was quiet, no other sound
Broke the silence of the singsing ground.

And ever the great drum beat, and beat,
And ever the woman sang.

Now was the time of sacrifice;
A cock was bound in a strange device
That only a savage could contrive,
Where he was slowly roasted alive.
A kid came next, a cow, a goat,
Then a spectacle on which to gloat—
A goat without horns, an offering dear,
Caught where a *blanc* may not appear
And guilty of killing the Sacred Snake
Sacrosanct for Obeah's sake—
A man in khaki was proudly led
To where the fire burned fiercely red;
There starved and weak he firmly stood
Before the priest in the singing wood.

And ever the great drum beat, and beat,
And ever the woman sang.

His staring eyes were open wide;
His broken arms hung by his side;
With death before him, fiendish, grim,
Never a whimper came from him,
Never a murmur, never a moan,
His heart within him cold as a stone.

And ever the great drum beat, and beat,
And ever the woman sang.

He uttered no useless plea or cry,
Silent he waited his time to die;
Only his blue eyes bulged and stared,
Stared, and stared, and stared, and stared,
As they laid him down on the gleaming fire
That was become his funeral pyre.
The voodoo priest performed the rite
Of sacrifice for the full moonlight.

And ever the great drum beat, and beat,
And ever the woman sang.

The head witch doctor, Almazo
Led their song, Oh-o-ay-o-eyah-oh,
And to its rhythm led the files about
In a savage serpentine, in and out;
The song became a barbaric paean,
Oh-o-ay-o-eyah, again and again.
High over the fires they leaped and sped;
In the crimson glare black flesh shone red.
The high moon shining silver where
It fell on their skins, sweating and bare.

And ever the great drum beat, and beat,
And ever the woman sang.

[Taken from Calland's *Voodoo* (New York: Harold Vinal, 1926). Text provided by Henry J. Vester.]

Articles

The Poets of *Weird Tales:* Part 2

Frank Coffman

The Great Triumvirate: Howard, Lovecraft, and Smith

Robert Ervin Howard, founder of the sword-and-sorcery genre of fantasy, fictioneer across several genres of popular imaginative literature, was a young man who, by his own claim, "splashed the field" across the spectrum of pulp fiction to make a living. Howard's poems in *Weird Tales* are an interesting sampling of the variety and virtuosity of that literary prodigy.

Howard was the best narrative poet of the triumvirate, one of the last proponents of story verse. While Lovecraft occasionally hits the mark and is undoubtedly a gifted versifier, his narrative poems often fall short in impact. The sonnets from the *Fungi from Yuggoth* sequence, with only a few exceptions, try to squeeze the horrific into too small a space. Smith was the consummate poet, most schooled in poetics and most polished and, by far, the most prolific of the three, but he stands apart and above principally in his lyric and self-expressive poems. Howard had the knack of presenting power and pace of action to the reader in perfectly metered and quickly and easily readable lines with almost no dependence on syntactical variation. As the youngest of the three, and despite his frequent claims in letters to Lovecraft and others that he had not studied poetry formally, his own poetic range and evident skill show a great understanding of poetic tradition, technique, and forms—especially if, as he claimed, he was self-taught.

Of the thirty-seven poems contributed by Howard to the early run of *Weird Tales*, eleven are sonnets, thus displaying Howard's love of and interest in that traditional form, considered the litmus test of the true poet's skill—at least at versifying—across all the languages of the West since the Italian Renaissance.

"Easter Island" (December 1928), published when he was only twenty-two and at the height of his intense poetry-writing period (which, amazingly, spanned only the years from his late teens through mid-twenties), is a descriptive and musing Italian sonnet (with irregular sestet) illustrating Howard's frequently seen theme of wanderlust and his definite yearning for both seafaring in particular and adventurous travel in general—beyond the imaginative wanderings at which he so excelled. Exotic places appealed greatly to Howard:

> How many weary centuries have flown
> Since strange-eyed beings walk this ancient shore,
> Hearing, as we, the green Pacific's roar,
> Hewing fantastic gods from sullen stone! . . .
> But now, they reign o'er a forgotten land,
> Gazing forever out beyond the tide.

"Moon Mockery" (April 1929) is a regular Italian sonnet and a poem about reincarnation (or at least ghostly lingering) set in the Ireland of Howard's great historical interest and imagined heritage. The wanderer reaches for and briefly holds "a slender moon" personified. But upon descending the Hill of Tara, he is much surprised. There are echoes of Rip Van Winkle's long and mystical sleep as well.

> I walked in Tara's wood one summer night, . . .
> And I went down the hill in opal light.
> And soon I was aware, as down I came,
> That all was strange and new on every side;
> Strange people went about me to and fro,
> And when I spoke with trembling mine own name
> They turned away, but one man said: "He died
> In Tara Wood, one hundred years ago."

One of Howard's best poems to appear in *Weird Tales* is "Recompense" (posthumously, November 1938), which displays his appreciation of fantasy and also his great love of and respect for the power of the imagination. It is in one of his favorite forms, what the present writer calls a "long-line ballad." Rather than using the 4343 pattern of the traditional ballad, Howard writes long seven-beat lines that look like rhymed couplets with internal rhyme, but are actually four plus three—the ballad stanza in disguise:

> I have not heard lutes beckon me, nor the brazen bugles call,
> But once in the dim of all haunted lea I heard the silence fall.
> I have not heard the regal drum, or seen the flags unfurled,
> But I have watched the dragons come, fire-eyed across the world. . . .
> I have not seen the face of Pan, nor mocked the dryad's haste,
> But I have trailed the dark-eyed man across a windy waste.
> I have not died as men may die, nor sin has been have sinned,
> But I have reached a misty sky upon a granite wind.

Another significant poem by Howard and another of his best is "The Hills of Kandahar" (posthumously, June/July 1939). Interestingly prophetic, it focuses upon Afghanistan, the place that was unconquerable by Alexander, by the British, and by the Russians. It remains to be seen what history will note of America's involvement there. The young Texan succinctly notes the significance of the place:

> The night primeval breaks in scarlet mist;
> The shadows gray, and pales each silent star,
> The eastern sky that rose-lipped dawn has kissed
> Glows crimson o'er the hills of Kandahar. . . .
> They will be brooding when mankind is gone;
> The teeming tribes that scaled their barricades—
> Dim hoards that waxed at dusk and waned at dawn—
> Are but as snow that on their shoulders fades.

Howard's views on poetry itself—at least on poetry considered in one of his darker moods—are outlined in "Which Will Scarcely Be Understood" (posthumously, October 1937). It begins: "Small poets sing a little foolish things . . .":

> True rime concerns her not with bursting buds,
> The chirping bird, the lifting of the rose—
> Save ebon blooms that swell in ghastly woods,

And that grim, voiceless bird that ever broods
Were through black boughs a wind of horror blows. . . .
Break down the altars, let the streets run red,
Tramp down the race into the crawling slime;
Then where red chaos lifts her serpent head,
The Fiend be praised, we'll pen the perfect rime.

Howard was much influenced by G. K. Chesterton's poetry and, specifically, *The Ballad of the White Horse*,[2] and he would use several stanzas of it for epigraphs for story or chapter headings in his prose. Like Chesterton, he adapted and modified the traditional four-line stanzas of the ballad of tradition into occasional fives and sixes, while keeping the essences of the short line rhythms of the troubadours.

In a letter to T. C. Smith somewhere around September of 1927, Howard wrote: "Several books I purchased on my trip, among them G. K. Chesterton's 'The Ballad of the White Horse'. Ever read it? It's great. Listen: . . ."[3] The fact that Howard would use the word "Listen" here is, I believe, a clear indication of his acute sense of the bardic nature of narrative verse and his belief that poetry was primarily meant to be heard and not "seen." This auditory sense helped make him the premier narrative poet of the triumvirs.

Howard's close friend, Tevis Clyde Smith, remembering Howard in the introduction to a slim chapbook of his friend's verse, wrote that "he was, certainly at the very first, primarily a poet."[4] Sadly, of course, there were not many years for Howard after "the very first." In the same degree that his appreciators mourn the loss of the great prose fiction that might have been, so should we regret the early loss of Howard's poetic voice, showing so great an early mastery and untold potential.

2. One of the last great poems in the epic tradition in English, surpassed perhaps only by William Morris's *Sigurd the Volsung and the Fall of the Niblungs*.

3. Robert E. Howard, *Selected Letters: 1923–30*, ed. Glenn Lord et al. (West Warwick, RI: Necronomicon Press, 1989).

4. Tevis Clyde Smith, "Introduction" to *The Grim Land and Others*, ed. Jonathan Bacon (Lamoni, IA: Stygian Isle Press, 1976), n.p.

It was certainly true that Howard yearned to be successful with his poetry and hoped to get it published more broadly. But the market and chance of profitability, then as now, wasn't there for verse, and the young man turned his attention to the prose fiction that paid the bills over the last years of his short life. Only twenty poems of his total count of thirty-seven were published in *Weird Tales* prior to his death. He was driven by the far greater market for his prose and the dearth of a market for verse, as he noted in the last poem to appear in the magazine during his lifetime, "Autumn" (April 1933): "Now is the lyre of Homer flecked with rust,/And yellow leaves are blown across the world . . ." Howard's poetry is much more extensive than most enthusiasts for his fiction realize. We have over 700 complete poems and fragments. These have been published in recent years in The Robert E. Howard Foundation's *The Collected Poetry of Robert E. Howard* (currently out of print); an extensive selection appeared as *Robert E. Howard: Selected Poems*.

H. P. Lovecraft, by most accounts, set a goal for himself to be the twentieth century's Poe, acknowledged literary voice in prose fiction, in poetry, and in critical commentary. While there is little doubt that Lovecraft's weird fiction achieves that goal and, indeed, surpasses the work of his great predecessor in many individual tales, especially the truly weird and supernaturally evocative works that are the foundation and early development of the Cthulhu Mythos; while the sheer enormity of his influence as a commentator and critic and mentor through the vastness of his epistolary output clearly establishes him as the most influential voice in the realms of supernatural horror in the early century; as a poet, he falls distinctly short of Poe. But this is not too great a condemnation, since one can have a great appreciation of and ear for language, be a more than competent versifier, and display significant virtuosity, inventiveness, and imagination, and still not reach the heights of poetic skill and achievement of one of America's greatest poets. And all these aforementioned virtues Lovecraft had. He displays these skills and his keen sense of poetic tradition in a poem on Poe, "Where Once Poe Walked" (May 1938), in the form of an abbreviated "acrostic sonnet"[5] capturing the essence of HPL's respect for his inspirer:

5. This "sonnet" is only 13 lines long, but it can rightly be called an

Lonely and sad, his spectre glides along
Aisles where of old his living footsteps fell;
No common glance discerns him, tho' his song
Peels down thro' time with a mysterious spell:
Only the few who sorcery's secret know:
Espy amidst these tombs the shade of Poe.

Lovecraft's best-known poems included in *Weird Tales* are from the *Fungi from Yuggoth* sequence of sonnets. Of the thirty-six poems in the sequence, twenty-seven were published in "The Unique Magazine." The sonnet sequence is one of the honored sub-traditions of this most ubiquitous fixed poetic form since its birth in the Italian Renaissance in the late thirteenth and early fourteenth centuries. It has been considered the mark of a true poet not only to work with the form, but most often— certainly through the nineteenth century—to write at least one sequence.

The problem with the form as a narrative unit, however, is its extreme brevity. The traditional sonnet is a lyric, self-expressive poem, originally on the theme of romantic love. But by the late eighteenth and early nineteenth centuries and thereafter, the sonnet form was adapted to a far greater diversity of themes and even redirected in mode so that the story sonnet began to emerge.

Poe nicely defines the "short tale"—what today we call the modern "short story"—in his seminal essay on Hawthorne's *Twice-Told Tales*, as a tale able to be read "in a single sitting" and creating a "single, unified effect upon the reader" with all included elements contributing to that effect. In that same important piece of criticism he notes a problem with extreme brevity:

> *A poem too brief may produce a vivid, but never an intense or enduring impression. Without a certain continuity of effort—without a certain duration or repetition of purpose—the soul is never deeply moved.* There must be the dropping of the water upon the rock. De Béranger has

---

"abbreviated sonnet" due to the number of letters in EDGARAL/LANPOE as the first letters of the lines spell out, but splitting AL/LAN to form the final sestet further indicated by the lack of division of stanzas as the three names would dictate normally in the acrostic.

wrought brilliant things—pungent and spirit-stirring—but, like all immassive bodies, they lack momentum, and thus fail to satisfy the Poetic Sentiment. They sparkle and excite, but, from want of continuity, fail deeply to impress. *Extreme brevity will degenerate into epigrammatism . . .*[6] (emphasis added)

And this is the problem with several of the individual "micro-stories" in Lovecraft's *Fungi* sequence: it is immensely difficult for the small square of poetry that is the sonnet to elicit an "intense or enduring impression" as a narrative. This is not to say that the task is impossible, simply that it is rarely successful. What works best is something more like what Lovecraft begins with in *Fungi*—a short series of sonnets, working much like stanzas or paragraphs that begin and continue a narrative through several poems. This is what Pushkin does with his novel written entirely in sonnets, *Evgenie Onegin*. In this manner, Lovecraft begins his sequence with the frame narrative of the theft of the book for forbidden mysteries and the pursuit from the old bookstore. The first five poems in *Fungi from Yuggoth* provide a frame for the chiefly micro-narratives and a few lyric musings to follow. Unfortunately, only the fifth of these "set-up" poems, "Homecoming" (1944, seven years after Lovecraft's death) was available to *Weird Tales* readers, and it was published late as well as out of sequence.

Of the narrative sonnets from *Fungi*, the most successful in achieving an "intense or enduring impression" are those that attempt the effect of shocking imagery such as "The Courtyard" (September 1930), depicting headless and handless walking corpses, or those that primarily attempt to develop an atmosphere of the supernatural without any significant narrative content, such as "Hesperia" (October 1930). A few of Lovecraft's narrative sonnets achieve the desired compacted effect. "Antarktos" (Nov. 1930) is one such poem:

> Deep in my dream the great bird whispered queerly
> Of the black cone amid the polar waste;
> Pushing above the ice-sheet lone and drearly,
> By storm-crazed aeons battered and defaced. . . .

6. Poe, "Review of *Twice-Told Tales* By Nathaniel Hawthorne," *Graham's Magazine* (May 1842): 298–99.

But the bird told of vaster parts, that under
The mile-deep ice-shroud crouch and brood and bide.
God help the dreamer whose mad visions shew
Those dead eyes set in crystal gulfs below!

And in "The Elder Pharos" (February/March 1931) Lovecraft gives a nod to one of his literary influences, Robert W. Chambers and *The King in Yellow,* and nicely amplifies the horrific aspects suggested by the saffron monarch's originator:

The Thing, they whisper, wears a silken mask
Of yellow; whose queer folds appear to hide
A face not of this earth, though none dares ask
Just what those features are, which bulge inside.

Lovecraft's best poems to appear in *Weird Tales* are in rhymed couplets and extend for many lines. This form is the historically dominant mode of narrative presentation in English verse, and Lovecraft shows great dexterity with it. In both "The Ancient Track" (March 1930) and "Psychopompos" (September 1937) he skillfully narrates poems much more in keeping with Poe's precepts about sufficient length for effect.

"Aletheia Phrikodes" (ancient Greek for "frightful truth," July 1952)[7] is subtitled in Latin: "*Omnia risus et omnia pulvis et omnia nihil*" ("All is laughter, all is dust, all is nothing"). The poem is in unrhymed iambic pentameter (blank verse), another widespread narrative form, since regular metrical cadence alone is required. This same meter, of course, is the measure of Shakespeare's plays, Milton's *Paradise Lost,* and many other classics of our literature. Lovecraft displays great virtuosity with the form and, in this poem, also displays his early-developed mindset:

. . . Borne on the wings of stark immensity
A touch of rhythm celestial reached my soul;
Thrilling me more with horror than with joy.

---

7. An extract from "The Poe-et's Nightmare," originally published in the *Vagrant* (July 1918).

Without doubt, Clark Ashton Smith was the most complete and, likely, the finest poet to find publication in *Weird Tales*. Not only was his the most often included poetic voice in "The Unique Magazine," but the uniform quality, amazing variety, richness of expression, and breadth and depth of his poetic art stand out in bold contrast to the efforts of the minor poets and versifiers who form the bulk of the magazine's other contributors.

Having said that, Smith's poetry is not for everyone. Smith would very likely agree by pointing out that he was not writing for everyone. Clark Ashton Smith was befriended and mentored by George Sterling, who himself had been the protégé of Ambrose Bierce. Sterling's important poem, "A Wine of Wizardry" (published in *Cosmopolitan* in 1907, broadly panned by "serious critics" of the day and those influenced by the modernist movement then in vogue, and, subsequently, even more vehemently and more effectively defended by Bierce) is the seminal poetic jewel of both the "Pure Poetry," Romantic-revivalist school of the early twentieth century and a defense of the legitimacy of the poetry of the fantastic, the sublime, and the supernatural. The lushness of its imagery and the richness of its figurative expression are only matched by its inclusion of archaisms and obscure diction. Most readers, even those who consider themselves great readers of poetry with extensive vocabularies, cannot read Smith (or Sterling, or, to a somewhat lesser degree, Smith's own protégés, Donald Wandrei and Donald Sidney-Fryer) without frequently resorting to a dictionary for clarification of the lush and intoxicating, but decidedly rare words encountered in almost every poem. But to lovers of the mystical power of language and the joy of words in themselves, this can be a great virtue. In his first poem to find inclusion in the magazine, "The Garden of Evil" (July/August 1923)—which, as noted above, is also the first verse by anyone to grace its pages—we have the following words: *mandragoras, bergamot. fumitory, langours, aconite, proffered,* and *phantasmal.* In the other poem to appear in that same issue, "The Red Moon," we see an example of a poem that we might say is "thematically targeted" to fulfill the kind of verse thought of as appropriate for *Weird Tales*—either story poems that present the weird and supernatural occurrence or poems that evoke a mood or atmosphere in keeping with the magazine's title and typical prose fiction content. "The Red Moon" is brief enough to include in its entirety here:

> The hills, a-throng with swarthy pine,
> Press up the pale and hollow sky,
> And the squat cypresses on high
> Reach from the lit horizon line.
>
> They reach, they reach, with gnarled hands—
> Malignant hags, obscene and dark—
> While the red moon, a demon's ark,
> Is borne along the mystic lands.

On the other hand, many of the poems to appear in *Weird Tales* are neither "weird" nor, quite often, are they "tales." Especially with Smith, I believe that Farnsworth Wright and the editors of the magazine simply wanted to include quality poetry when possible. Some of Smith's poems to appear in the magazine are best described as romantic lyrics. The poem "Sonnet" (April 1929) is simply a classic Italian-form love sonnet, a would-be lover's complaint. Or with "Ennui" (May 1936), an interesting variant Italian sonnet done in iambic hexameters, we have, again, a lyrical lover's complaint—with the only "weird" embedded in the almost Metaphysical conceits to be found in its unusual metaphors and images. But many of Smith's poems are far removed from and far above the typical verses to be found in *Weird Tales* by *hoi polloi* contributors about ghosts, goblins, monstrous creatures, things that go bump, or places that madden.

Smith contributed the best of the elegiac poems upon the death of his pen-friend, Lovecraft, "To Howard Phillips Lovecraft" (July 1937). The poem is written in random line lengths with random rhymes and shows Smith's keen sense of the traditional form of the elegy—from mourning the loss, to realization of the aspects of the person that remain, to consolation:

> . . . How far thy feet are sped
> Upon the fabulous and mooted ways
> Where walk the mythic dead!
> For us the grief, for us the mystery . . .

And yet thou art not gone . . .
I meet some wise and sentient wraith of thee,
Some undeparting presence, gracious and august . . .
And in the mind thou art for ever shown
As in a wizard glass,
And from the spirit's page thy runes can never pass.

Over the course of his poetic contributions to *Weird Tales*, Smith only repeats a poetic form or rhyme pattern three times across more than forty poems, not counting his translations from the French of Baudelaire and Verlaine. He was a great experimenter with poetic form, and his experiments are nearly always magnificent excursions into the ways form and content can meld.

In one of his best poems for the magazine, "Song of the Necromancer" (February 1937), Smith captures, in the very first stanza, much of what both his weird poetry and his weird fiction are able to convey:

I will repeat a subtle rune—
And thronging suns of Otherwhere
Shall blaze upon the blinded air,
And spectres terrible and fair
Shall walk the riven world at noon.

Some Other Contributors of Significance

Likely the best poet to contribute to *Weird Tales* after the "Triumvirate" was Smith's protégé Donald Wandrei. Continuing in the "Pure Poetry" traditions of the English Romantics and of Sterling and Smith, Wandrei's poems are luxurious and sonorous and mellifluous, filled with memorable images and striking metaphors. More so than any other frequent contributor to the magazine, Wandrei's submissions were almost always "on target" in presenting the weird and horrific. Clearly, he wrote much of his material "to the market" and knew what the editors were seeking. Like Lovecraft, Wandrei contributed a sonnet sequence, *Sonnets of the Midnight Hours*, the best poem from which is perhaps "Doom" (February 1929), a bleak vision of the end of all things:

Oblivion had lain its deathless curse
Upon all things of life and time and space;
Of death itself, there now was left no trace,
And DOOM had fallen on the universe.

The two most successfully contributing woman poets were without question Dorothy Quick and Leah Bodine Drake. Each had twenty-four poems in the magazine. Quick is best known as the author of *Mark Twain and Me*. She was the first of what was to become the cadre of Twain's "Angelfish," as he called them, young girls between ten and sixteen whom Clemens sought to mentor as writers.[8] Drake's eventual published collection, *A Hornbook for Witches*, is one of the rare and supremely collectible Arkham House publications with only 553 copies, 300 given to Drake herself. Both poets contributed verses of merit, most often on theme with the typical content of the magazine.

Publishing under the pseudonym of A. Leslie, the successful western and adventure writer Alexander Leslie Scott contributed twenty-three poems to *Weird Tales*. Robert E. Howard was particularly enthusiastic about the quality of his work.

All in all, for the scope of this article, there are far too many interesting poems and interesting poets to consider that found their way into the pages of the magazine. An anthology of *all* the verse to appear in "The Unique Magazine" would be an important contribution to pulp and popular literature studies. The entirety of the poetry collected as a chronological compilation, with alternative tables of contents by authors, forms, and themes, is a project well worth undertaking.

The *Weird Tales* poems by Howard, Lovecraft, and Smith have already been extracted and compiled, enabling both appreciation and close study, but a major volume of the entirety of the poetry from "The Unique Magazine" is called for. Howard's skills with poetic narrative, capturing both the pace and power of his fantastic and supernatural

8. The "Angelfish" group should not be interpreted as in any way scandalous. Clemens had lost two daughters and his wife in the span of little more than a decade, and these associations were likely completely innocent, perhaps fulfilling a fatherly as well as mentoring impulse. Certainly there is no hint of anything inappropriate in Quick's *Mark Twain and Me*.

prose fiction; Lovecraft's virtuosity with verse, and especially his nuances with the sonnet form used as both lyric and narrative; and the broad range, thematic diversity, and astounding acumen of Smith's poetics are, in themselves, reasons enough for such an anthology. And the many currently obscure, if not effectively "lost," poetic voices of merit might be heard again.

I hope that this brief introductory might prove to be useful, both in stimulating interest in the reader for further investigation of the poetry of *Weird Tales*, and, beyond that, might be the first step along the way to encouraging the compilation of such an anthology—one that would gather the scattered and barely accessible "leaves" of such a forest.

Note of Thanks

I must add a sincere note of thanks to friends and scholars who helped me in the daunting task of assembling a good portion of the obscure poetry of *Weird Tales*. Special thanks to Scotty Henderson, who steered me to many digital reprints and facsimiles of early issues and to Morgan Holmes, who excavated and published a plethora of early *Weird Tales* verses in the REHupa mailing list subsequent to my plea for help.

Reviews

The Generalist and the Specialist

S. T. Joshi

WILLIAM F. NOLAN. *Soul Trips: Collected Poems 1940–2015.*
Vancouver, WA: Cycatrix Press, 2015. 98 pp. $14.95 tpb.
BRETT RUTHERFORD. *Trilobite Love Song: Selected Poems & Revisions,
2013–2014.* Providence, RI: The Poet's Press, 2014. 55 pp. $8.95 tpb.

Readers have not always been kind to *diverse* authors—authors who do not specialize in a single genre or a single literary mode. Such authors become difficult to pigeonhole, often unfairly typecast by a celebrated work ("Robert Bloch, author of *Psycho*") that is taken to represent the totality of their output. William F. Nolan (b. 1928), has not been exempt from this stereotyping: he must now be unutterably weary of being branded "the author [in fact, he is the coauthor] of *Logan's Run,*" a label that does grave disservice to him as a writer of supernatural horror, crime fiction, science fiction, and—outside the realm of prose fiction—of biographies (Steve McQueen, John Huston, among others), and, as we now find in this slender but substantial booklet, of deft, moving poetry.

Nolan makes it clear in his introduction to *Soul Trips* that this is a scrupulous selection from the many hundreds of poems that he has been writing since the age of nine. The selection may in fact have been a little too judicious: based on the poems actually included, Nolan has probably written many more poems that would command interest today.

The volume should in no way be considered an "all-weird" collection; indeed, only a few poems could be considered such. And that is only fitting, given Nolan's range of interests. This book, indeed, poignantly hints at the breadth of his involvement with literature—and with writers—over a long life. His decades-long friendship with Ray Bradbury (now embodied in the award-winning volume *Nolan on*

Bradbury [Hippocampus Press, 2013]) is keenly etched in the touching "God Bless!," written for Bradbury's eightieth birthday. As a leading biographer on Dashiell Hammett, Nolan has written poems on Hammett and Chandler; his devotion to the prolific pulp writer Max Brand is exhibited in "Max Brand: Pulp King." "Final Exit" is a striking tribute to Sylvia Plath, written in her own searing poetic manner. But the longest and most impressive poem about an author is "Hemingway: Now Never There," a scintillating rumination on the American writer who himself was larger than life:

> The breathing woods no longer
> softly crackle
> to his quick Indian tread.
> No flushed quail rises,
> beating air;
> no cabin waits, warm-hearthed,
> on Walloon Lake.
> He is not there.

"Uncivil War" is an unforgettable poem about the bloodiest war in American history, one whose grim echoes still resound in our day. This point is further emphasized in the moving poem "My Father Called Them Darkies," a plangent tribute to a man whose unconscious and socially induced prejudice against African Americans did not preclude him from being a decent man ("My Father, / from Missouri, where blacks are hated, / had no hate in him").

Of the specifically horrific poems, it is impossible not to single out "Undead," a powerful vampire lyric:

> I seek the night
> in red hunger
> for how can my rich
> blood-dark dreams
> find substance
> in the horrors of full day?

"Dread Voyage" brings out the weirdness of classical myth in its account of a son of Aeneas who battles the sorceress Circe. "The Final Quest" shows King Arthur battling the redoubtable figure of Death—and apparently winning.

There is much more good work in this book, and no one ought to mistake its slender page-count for a lack of substance. It reveals the varied fruits of a long and variegated life—a life of constant intellectual and aesthetic exploration. And at the age of eighty-eight, William F. Nolan is by no means finished.

Brett Rutherford is the polar opposite of Nolan in many ways. He has, in his own long life (I imagine he is in his sixties), focused relentlessly and fruitfully on the writing, editing, and publishing of poetry, specifically weird poetry. *Trilobite Love Song* announces itself as the 209th publication of his Poet's Press, and a splendid little book it is.

Like Nolan, Rutherford prefers free verse—and, like his older contemporary, he recognizes that free verse requires even more care and attention than formal verse, and an even more concentrated fund of metaphor, symbolism, and imagery to qualify as true verse rather than as unrhymed prose. The instances where Rutherford's occasional penchant for conversational verse in the William Carlos Williams manner—a form not very distinguishable from prose, in my estimation—are, in this small book, mercifully few. Instead, we have potent vignettes such as "A Year and a Day," an extraordinarily poignant poem about "obsessive love":

> I thought the sun, unbent by atmosphere,
> would melt your cold heart;
> the rain that came
> we mistook for a sign of advent—
> o roots, o tendrils, o new shoots twining,
> abandoned as abruptly
> to summer's drought,
> to hoarfrost cold,
> and now, to this barren anniversary.

A good many of the poems will be a delight to Lovecraftians—not surprisingly from one who lived for many years in Lovecraft's Providence, Rhode Island. "The Shadow over Innsmouth" seems to be of particular fascination to Rutherford, and several poems tease out the latent suggestions of aberrant sex, social alienation, and biological anomaly latent in that story. The evocative final section of "At Innsmouth Harbor" can only be quoted:

> There is no catalog of flotsam, no list
> of the things that will not come to shore:
> the ten-lobed all-seeing eyes of the ghosts
> of Trilobites, mandarins of the ocean deep;
> the wary, watchful ammoniac waiting
> of Architeuthis, the giant squid; the pound
> and beat of the tide-drum, counting all down
> to the world's end, the sun's death, the pull
> of all into the dark heart of the iron stone
> where everything that was and will be comes to rest.

Analogously, "Providence Nocturne: Two Portraits" tells what it is like to be a Deep One. "On the Island of Pohnpei," referring to the island that Lovecraft in "The Shadow over Innsmouth" calls Ponape, speaks of that obscure realm becoming a tourist attraction ("There's a neon sign, oh, you'll see it, / with tacky Hawaiian lettering, that reads / LOUNGE R'LYEH–HOOKAH ALL NIGHT").

Rutherford quietly reveals both his learning and his range of poetic skills by presenting translations or paraphrases both from the Russian ("Alexander Pushkin: The Demons") and from the Chinese of Li Yü, the last emperor of Southern Tang, who died around 978 C.E.

In short, we here have two poets who, scorning the canard that poetry is dead in our time, have spent decades producing vital, compelling verse that commands our attention for its precision, its unforgettable collocation of words, and its reflection of two lifetimes' worth of ruminations on the human and the cosmic. And we are the beneficiaries of their devotion to the form and substance of poetry.

Leaves Grown Heavy with Omens

Wade German

ANN K. SCHWADER. *Dark Energies*. Preface by S. T. Joshi. Afterword by Robert M. Price. Edited by Charles Lovecraft. Sydney, Australia: P'rea Press, 2015. 110 pp. $14.50 AUD tpb.

If there is one thing we have learned in recent decades, it is that H. P. Lovecraft is the ultimate renewable energy source. His imaginative works have inspired innumerable fissions and fusions from latter-day writers, resulting in the Cyclopean cornucopia of Lovecraftiana that we have today. And if Lovecraftian fandom could be considered a cult, then it was long ago that Ann K. Schwader was anointed high priestess of the versifying sect.

Schwader writes with precision and often with elegance, and from territories where even the slightest breeze can evoke visions of the dark fantastic:

> Chill winds at midnight ripple cloth of gold:
> these draperies whose twisted arabesques
> suggest no single form, yet somehow hold
> a thousand shadows of the pure grotesque.

One always finds euphony in Schwader's lines, and her enjambments sometimes energize the sense of chaos or entropy that is so often part of her subject. She always approaches traditional poetic forms with understanding and the requisite skill, and many of the poems in this volume reveal an artist who has achieved even further refinements.

Prime examples are the startlingly strange "*Cordyceps zombii*" and the gleefully morbid "Lullaby for Arachnophobes," in which we might imagine the most awful stepmother in the world warbling to her horrible cuckoo-children at bedtime:

Remember children: spiders never sleep—

Their eyes are multiple, their thoughts are deep
Beyond the boundaries of human schemes.
Their webs stretch wide, & what the catch, they keep

Wrapped mummy-tight. You'd never make a peep
Although your bones were softening to cream.

Elsewhere, Schwader leads us into myth and mystery with well-honed hooks ("In this kingdom of the spirits, men are trees"). And pleasingly odd pictures abound, such as these—"three floating gray cauliflowers"—which are vivid enough on their own but especially macabre when the metaphor knocks.

I have never thought to recommend a soundtrack for a poem before, but one might want to put on *Symphonies of the Planets* (there are five volumes, any one of them will do) to accompany a reading of "Void Music."

Schwader excels with compressed narratives, exemplified in poems such as "The *Ba*-Curse":

They asked him if he feared the mummy's curse,
The blameless maid he'd stolen from her tomb.
The excavator laughed: he'd heard far worse
In every local *souk*. As twilight's gloom
Suffused the valley like the Nile at flood,
He lit a lamp & tied his tent-flaps tight,
Then with a flourish fit to freeze the blood,
He poured a dram & bade his prize good night.

*   *   *

They never knew what savaged him, although
He shrieked it very clearly as he died:
"Ba! Ba!" A madman's babble . . . even so,
His men won't speak of things they saw inside,
For neither time nor whiskey can erase
That black-winged nightmare with a maiden's face.

As a staunch Lovecraftian, Schwader's work is heavily informed by cosmicism, generally leaning toward pessimism rather than indifferentism. But even when the darkest areas of the human aquarium are under observation, she keeps things frosty, even clinically so, and never lets things ripen into the squishy sentimentalism so often found in the mainstream.

Dark Energies contains many homages to Lovecraft and other weird fiction giants such as Clark Ashton Smith, Robert W. Chambers, Edgar Allan Poe, and W. H. Pugmire. Steeped in mythoi, a few of these might seem a bit opaque to some readers, but those already familiarized with the source material will find much to savor and appreciate.

Sex and Sin

Sunni K Brock

STEPHANIE M. WYTOVICH. *Brothel.* Bowie, MD: Raw Dog Screaming Press, 2016. 172 pages. $14.95 tpb.

Stephanie M. Wytovich has earned her place as a leading voice in horror poetry. Her latest collection, *Brothel,* is a delightful collection of verse in which she invites the readers to indulge their fantasies and fears, no matter how dark, perverse, or disturbing.

As the title implies, sex and sin play a central role in the dark themes explored, but it's not just debauchery that makes this collection intriguing. Wytovich imbues each poem with a soul of its own: each a small story, each a complexity of emotion beautiful and raw, yet with verse so refined, you hardly notice the depth of the cut until you are bleeding out in awe.

To quote "Dirty Sheets":

> There's blood on my bed
> from the tears that I've cried,
> every time you took me,
> every time I died.

Indeed, every page of the one hundred sixty-nine entries in this volume is a *petite mort,* enough to satisfy over and over.

Notes on Contributors

Carole Abourjeili started writing poetry in Arabic and French in Lebanon; then, a few years after migrating to Australia at age twelve, she began writing in English. Most of her poems deal with the supernatural and what lies beyond the known: "Each poem is a piece of my soul that I like to share with the world. For me, writing is a place where I find inner peace and connection with the Divine."

Ross Balcom lives in southern California. His poems have appeared in *Beyond Centauri, inkscrawl, Poetry Midwest, Scifaikuest, Star*Line,* and other publications. He is a frequent contributor to *Songs of Eretz Poetry Review.*

David Barker has been a fan of weird literature all his life. Recently, his writings have appeared in *Fungi, Cyäegha,* and *Shoggoth.net.* In collaboration with W. H. Pugmire, David has had two books published by Dark Renaissance Books: *The Revenant of Rebecca Pascal* (2014) and *In the Gulfs of Dream and Other Lovecraftian Tales* (2015).

F. J. Bergmann writes poetry and speculative fiction, often simultaneously, appearing in *Apex, Cleaver, Forklift, Ohio, Grievous Angel, Helen,* and elsewhere, and functioning, so to speak, as editor of *Star*Line,* the journal of the Science Fiction Poetry Association, and poetry editor of *Mobius: The Journal of Social Change,* and managing editor of MadHat Press.

Leigh Blackmore has written weird verse since age thirteen. He has lived in the Illawarra, New South Wales, Australia, for the last decade. He has edited *Terror Australis: Best Australian Horror* (1993) and *Midnight Echo 5* (2011) and written *Spores from Sharnoth & Other Madnesses* (2008). A nominee for SFPA's Rhysling Award (Best Long Poem), Leigh is also a four-time Ditmar Award nominee. He is currently preparing a chapbook of his Sherlock Holmes stories entitled *Horrors of Sherlock Holmes.*

Adam Bolivar, a native of Boston, now residing in Portland, Oregon, has had his weird fiction and poetry appear in the pages of *Nameless,* the

Lovecraft eZine, *Spectral Realms*, and Chaosium's *Steampunk Cthulhu* and *Atomic Age Cthulhu* anthologies. His first book, *The Fall of the House of Drake*, was published by Dunhams Manor Press in 2015.

Sunni K Brock's fiction and poetry combines science fiction, horror, fantasy and erotica. As one-half of the team of JaSunni Productions, LLC and Cycatrix Press, she creates genre film and print with her husband, Jason. If she had spare time, she would pursue genealogy, shopping at the farmer's market, and conducting experiments on controlled randomness.

Jeff Burnett was first published in *Spectral Realms* #4. His influences are Clark Ashton Smith and Robert E. Howard. When not working, he spends his time writing poetry, playing mandolin, adventuring with his wife, and hunting the Ozark Highlands of Missouri.

G. O. Clark's writing has been published in *Asimov's Science Fiction*, *Analog*, *Space & Time*, *A Sea of Alone: Poems for Alfred Hitchcock*, *Tales of the Talisman*, *Daily SF*, *Jupiter* (GB) and more. He's the author of eleven poetry collections, most recently *Gravediggers' Dance* (2014). His fiction collection *Twists & Turns* (Alban Lake Publishing) came out in 2016. He was a Stoker Award finalist in poetry in 2011. He lives in Davis, California.

Frank Coffman is professor of English, journalism, and creative writing at Rock Valley College in Rockford, Illinois. His primary interests as a critic are in the rise and relevance of popular imaginative literature across the genres of adventures, detection and mystery, fantasy, horror and the supernatural, and science fiction. He has published several articles on these genres and is the editor of Robert E. Howard's *Selected Poems*.

Ashley Dioses is a writer of dark fiction and poetry from Southern California. She is currently working on her first book of weird poetry. Her poetry has appeared in *Weird Fiction Review*, *Spectral Realms*, *Xnoybis*, *Weirdbook*, *Gothic Blue Book*, Volume 5 (Burial Day Books, 2015), and elsewhere.

Ian **Futter** began writing stories and poems in his childhood, but only lately has started to share them. One of his poems appears in Jason V Brock's anthology *The Darke Phantastique* (Cycatrix Press, 2014), and he continues to produce dark fiction for admirers of the surreal.

Liam **Garriock** is a writer, poet, and eternal disciple of Arthur Machen, Algernon Blackwood, William Hope Hodgson, Edgar Allan Poe, H. P. Lovecraft, and M. R. James, with an interest in the fantastic and esoteric side of life and anything that revolts against the prosaic. He lives in Edinburgh, Scotland.

Wade **German**'s writings have appeared in journals such as *Fungi, Hypnos, Weirdbook, Weird Fiction Review,* and previous issues of *Spectral Realms.* His poetry has been nominated for the Pushcard, Rhysling, and Elgin awards and has received honorable mentions in Ellen Datlow's *Best Horror of the Year* anthologies. His collection *Dreams from a Black Nebula* was published by Hippocampus Press.

Juan J. **Gutiérrez** lives in Desert Hot Springs, California, with his loving wife and daughters. His poetry and fiction have appeared in many anthologies and ezines, most recently in *Barbarian Crowns* and *Sinbad and the Wings of Destiny.*

Chad **Hensley** is a poet and author. His first book of poetry, *Embrace the Hideous Immaculate,* was published in May 2014 by Raw Dog Screaming Press. His recent poetry appearances include the *Horror Writers Association Horror Poetry Showcase III, Weirdbook* #31 and #32, and the first four issues of *Spectral Realms.* Look for a new version of his nonfiction book *EsoTerra: The Journal of Extreme Culture* later this year.

Jennifer **Ruth Jackson** writes about reality's weirdness and the plausibilities of the fantastic. Her work has appeared in *Strange Horizons, Star*Line, Apex Magazine,* and more. She lives in a small Wisconsin city with her husband.

S. T. **Joshi** has edited the poetical works of Clark Ashton Smith (2007-8), Donald Wandrei (2008), H. L. Mencken (2009), and George Sterling (2013), all for Hippocampus Press. His brief treatise *Emperors of Dreams:*

Some Notes on Weird Poetry was published in 2008 by P'rea Press. He has written many critical and biographical studies in the realm of weird fiction.

Gregory MacDonald is a twenty-five-year-old lover of all types of writing, from fantasy fiction to sci-fi poetry, and is located in Grass Valley, California. He has been writing for more than half a decade, and he draws his influences from the Romantic and Gothic traditions, chiefly, Percy Bysshe Shelley and George Sterling.

John J. Mundy's poems first appeared in *Spectral Realms*. His first published short story, a grim little tale of alchemy and the Black Pilgrimage, appears in the Mark Samuels tribute anthology *Marked for Death*, edited by the indefatigable Justin Isis. His literary heroes are H. P. Lovecraft, Jorge Luis Borges, and the late great Friedrich Dürrenmatt. He has considerable admiration for the macabre poetry of Joseph Payne Brennan while finding an unending source of inspiration in Lovecraft's wonderful *Fungi from Yuggoth*.

D. L. Myers's poetry has appeared in previous issues of *Spectral Realms*. His influences include H. P. Lovecraft, Clark Ashton Smith, Robert E. Howard, George Sterling, Algernon Blackwood, and Arthur Machen. He dwells among the mist-shrouded hills and farms of the Skagit Valley in the Pacific Northwest with his partner and a pack of demon badger hounds.

Charles D. O'Connor III is a thirty-three-year-old prose poet of the strange residing in Virginia. This issue of *Spectral Realms* marks his second appearance and his fifth prose piece published overall. He is making his mark slowly but surely. The poem appearing here he dedicates, first, to his late father Charles O'Connor Jr., dear late friend Dr. William C. Farmer, and his ancestor Dr. Robert Thornton, famous botanist.

K. A. Opperman is a poet with a predilection for the strange, the Gothic, and the grotesque, continuing the macabre and fantastical tradition of such luminaries as Poe, Clark Ashton Smith, and H. P. Lovecraft. His first verse collection, *The Crimson Tome*, was published by Hippocampus Press in 2015.

Fred Phillips's first collection of poetry, *From the Cauldron*, was published by Hippocampus Press in 2010; a second collection, *Winds from Sheol*, is under way. He has been published in the *Cimmerian*, *Studies in the Fantastic*, *Weird Fiction Review*, and elsewhere.

W. H. Pugmire likes to follow Poe's example and plant poetry into his weird fiction. His sonnet sequence, "Songs of Sesqua Valley," appeared in *Sesqua Valley and Other Haunts* (Delirium Books, 2003). He is now at work on "Sonnets of an Eldritch Bent."

Joseph S. Pulver, Sr. has released four mixed-genre collections, a collection of *King in Yellow* tales, two novels, and edited *A Season in Carcosa*, the Shirley Jackson Award–winning *The Grimscribe's Puppets*, and *Cassilda's Song*. His fiction and poetry have appeared in many notable anthologies, including *Autumn Cthulhu*, *The Children of Old Leech*, Ellen Datlow's *The Year's Best Horror*, *The Book of Cthulhu*, *A Mountain Walked*, and *Best Weird Fiction of the Year*.

A native of northwest Indiana, **Nathaniel Reed**'s work heavily reflects and draws from this locale, often borrowing settings from the dunes and marshes surrounding Lake Michigan. He currently studies biology and education at Purdue Northwest and will soon be graduating and beginning his career as a high school teacher. He thanks Whitney Wilmoth for her early readings and encouragement.

Ann K. Schwader lives and writes in Colorado. Her most recent collections are *Dark Energies* (P'rea Press, 2015) and *Twisted in Dream* (Hippocampus Press, 2011). Her *Wild Hunt of the Stars* (Sam's Dot, 2010) and *Dark Energies* were Bram Stoker Award finalists. She is also a 2010 Rhysling Award winner, and was the Poet Laureate for NecronomiCon Providence 2015.

Darrell Schweitzer's two serious poetry collections are *Groping toward the Light* and *Ghosts of Past and Future*. He hopes to have a third, exclusively weird collection out soon. His next book will be *The Threshold of Forever*, a collection of essays and reviews. He used to edit *Weird Tales*.

John Shirley is the author of numerous novels and books of short stories. His latest novel is *Doyle After Death* (HarperCollins, 2013), a tale of Sir Arthur Conan Doyle in the afterlife. He won the Bram Stoker Award for his story collection *Black Butterflies*.

Oliver Smith's writing has appeared in anthologies published by the Inkerman Press, Ex Occidente Press, and Dark Hall Press.

Christina Sng is a Rhysling-nominated poet and writer. Her work has received several honorable mentions in *The Year's Best Fantasy and Horror*. She is the author of three chapbooks, and her first full-length book of poetry, *A Collection of Nightmares*, is slated for late 2016 from Raw Dog Screaming Press.

Verse by Providence native **Jonathan Thomas** has consisted mostly of lyrics for country singer Angel Dean, Manhattan bands Escape by Ostrich and Fish & Roses, Swedish quartet scumCrown, and his own Septimania. His prose collections include *Midnight Call* (2008), *Tempting Providence* (2010), *Thirteen Conjurations* (2013), and *Dreams of Ys and Other Invisible Worlds* (2015), all from Hippocampus Press.

Richard L. Tierney's *Collected Poems* appeared from Arkham House in 1981. A later volume of poetry was published as *Savage Menace and Other Poems of Horror* (P'rea Press, 2010). Tierney is also the author of *The Winds of Zarr* (Silver Scarab Press, 1975), *The House of the Toad* (Fedogan & Bremer, 1993), and many other works of horror and fantasy fiction.

M. F. Webb recently returned to writing from a two-decade long, journalism-induced hiatus. Her poetry has appeared in previous issues of *Spectral Realms*, and her fiction in *Latchkey Tales*. A Texas transplant, she has made her home in Seattle for the past seventeen years. Her great-great-great-grandmother was a Poe.

Mary Krawczak Wilson has written poetry, fiction, plays, articles, and essays. She was born in St. Paul, Minnesota, and moved to Seattle in 1991. Her most recent essay appeared in the *American Rationalist*.

CPSIA information can be obtained
at www.ICGtesting.com
Printed in the USA
FSOW02n0900170916
25131FS